I0799658

COMFORT MADE **DELICIOUS**

simple recipes for cozy classics

from the
HOFFMAN MEDIA TEST KITCHEN

83 press®

Copyright © 2026 by 83 Press

All rights reserved. No part of this book may be reproduced or transmitted in any form or by any means, electronic or mechanical, including photocopying, or by any information storage and retrieval system, without permission in writing from 83 Press. Reviewers may quote brief passages for specific inclusion in a magazine or newspaper.

83 Press
2323 2nd Avenue North
Birmingham, Alabama 35203
83press.com

ISBN 978-1-971708-90-4
Printed in China

83 press

COMFORT MADE DELICIOUS

simple recipes for cozy classics

CONTENTS

preface

When we crave comfort, we often turn to dishes that are nostalgic and remind us of home. Maybe it's chicken noodle soup from our grandmother's kitchen, or a memorable dessert made by friends every holiday. Regardless, these special meals give us that same easy feeling. Good food is more than just a meal; it's a reminder of where we began, or even a gentle guide toward where we're headed. One thing is for sure, comfort should be made delicious for everyone.

Within these pages, the Hoffman Media Test Kitchen gathers the dishes that bring them the most joy, from heartwarming soups to down-home suppers. The array of tastes and flavors that flows through this book will bring both familiar favorites and new bites that could become your next dinner tradition.

BREADS AND BITES

chapter 1

BUTTERMILK BISCUITS

MAKES 12

These perfect biscuits are rich, buttery, flaky, and ready for your favorite filling.

3½ cups all-purpose flour*
2 tablespoons sugar
1 tablespoon kosher salt
1 tablespoon baking powder
½ teaspoon baking soda
1¼ cups cold unsalted butter, cubed
1 cup cold whole buttermilk
1 large egg, lightly beaten
Flaked sea salt, for sprinkling
Butter and honey, to serve

1. Preheat oven to 425°. Line a baking sheet with parchment paper.
2. In a large bowl, whisk together flour, sugar, salt, baking powder, and baking soda. Using a pastry blender, cut in cold butter until mixture is crumbly. Stir in cold buttermilk until a shaggy dough forms.
3. Turn out dough onto a lightly floured surface. Pat dough into a rectangle, and cut into fourths. Stack each fourth on top of each other, and pat into a rectangle again. Repeat procedure 3 more times. Pat or roll dough to 1-inch thickness. Using a 2½-inch round cutter dipped in flour, cut dough without twisting cutter, rerolling scraps as necessary. Place biscuits 2 inches apart on prepared pan. Freeze until cold, about 10 minutes. Brush with egg, and sprinkle with sea salt.
4. Bake until golden brown, about 15 minutes. Serve with butter and honey.

**We used White Lily.*

CHEESE AND PEPPER STUFFED CORNBREAD

MAKES ABOUT 8 SERVINGS

A little heat and a lot of cheese pack this Southern classic with extra flavor.

- **1 cup all-purpose flour**
- **1 cup plain yellow cornmeal**
- **½ teaspoon kosher salt**
- **½ teaspoon baking soda**
- **2 large eggs**
- **1 cup whole buttermilk**
- **½ cup unsalted butter, melted**
- **3 tablespoons honey**
- **2 cups shredded Monterey Jack cheese with peppers, divided**
- **¼ teaspoon crushed red pepper**

1. Preheat oven to 375°. Spray a 9-inch cast-iron skillet with cooking spray.

2. In a large bowl, stir together flour, cornmeal, salt, and baking soda.

3. In a medium bowl, whisk together eggs, buttermilk, melted butter, and honey until smooth.

4. Make a well in center of flour mixture; add egg mixture, stirring just until combined. Spread half of batter in prepared skillet. Sprinkle with 1½ cups cheese. Spread remaining batter over cheese in an even layer. Do not stir. Sprinkle with red pepper and remaining ½ cup cheese.

5. Bake until golden brown, about 30 minutes. Let cool for 5 minutes before serving.

RUTABAGA ROLLS

MAKES 15

Mashed rutabaga creates a tender, sponge-like texture in these rolls and keeps them moist while the flavor of the root itself is mild.

- **3¼ to 3½ cups bread flour, divided**
- **¼ cup sugar**
- **1 (0.25-ounce) package active dry yeast**
- **1¼ teaspoons kosher salt**
- **½ cup plus 1 tablespoon whole milk, divided**
- **6 tablespoons unsalted butter, softened**
- **½ cup mashed cooked rutabaga (see Kitchen Tip)**
- **2 large eggs, divided**
- **1 tablespoon unsalted butter, melted**
- **Everything bagel seasoning, for sprinkling**

1. In the bowl of a stand mixer fitted with the paddle attachment, combine 1 cup flour, sugar, yeast, and salt until well combined.

2. In a medium saucepan, combine ½ cup milk and butter; cook over medium heat until butter is melted and an instant-read thermometer registers 120° to 130°. Add milk mixture to flour mixture; beat on medium speed for 2 minutes. Add rutabaga and 1 egg; beat on medium-high speed for 2 minutes. Gradually add 2¼ cups flour, beating until just combined. Switch to the dough hook attachment; beat on medium speed for 10 to 12 minutes, adding remaining ¼ cup flour, 1 tablespoon at a time, until a soft, smooth, elastic dough forms. Scrape down sides of bowl and dough hook, as needed.

3. Coat a large bowl with cooking spray. Place dough in bowl, turning to grease top. Cover and let rise in a warm, draft-free place (75°) until doubled in size, 40 minutes to 1 hour.

4. Line a rimmed baking sheet with parchment paper.

5. Punch dough down. Turn out dough onto a lightly floured surface and divide into 15 pieces and shape into balls. Place rolls on prepared baking sheet. Cover and let rise in a warm, draft-free place (75°) until doubled in size, 40 minutes to 1 hour.

6. Preheat oven to 375°.

7. In a small bowl, whisk together remaining 1 egg and remaining 1 tablespoon milk; brush over rolls.

8. Bake until golden brown and an instant-read thermometer inserted in center registers at least 190°, about 15 minutes.

9. Brush rolls with melted butter. Sprinkle with everything bagel seasoning. Serve warm.

KITCHEN TIP For mashed rutabaga, combine 1 cup diced rutabaga and cold water to cover by 1 inch in a medium saucepan. Bring to a boil, reduce to a simmer, and cook until tender, 30 to 45 minutes. Drain and let stand until dry. Transfer rutabaga to the work bowl of a food processor and pulse until smooth, scraping down sides, if needed. Let cool completely before using in rolls.

CLOVERLEAF ROLLS

MAKES ABOUT 24

Fluff and buttery, these are the perfect companion to any meal. Try topping these rolls with grated Parmesan for a cheesy twist.

- 2 cups warm water (105° to 110°)
- ⅔ cup instant nonfat dry milk
- ¼ cup plus 1 teaspoon sugar, divided
- 1 (0.25-ounce) package active dry yeast
- 6 cups all-purpose flour, divided
- ⅓ cup plus 2 tablespoons unsalted butter, melted and divided
- 1 large egg
- 2 teaspoons kosher salt
- 1 tablespoon coarse sea salt
- 1 tablespoon poppy seeds

1. In the bowl of a stand mixer fitted with the paddle attachment, combine 2 cups warm water, dry milk, and 1 teaspoon sugar. Add yeast, and let stand until mixture is foamy, about 10 minutes.

2. With mixer on medium speed, add 2 cups flour, ⅓ cup melted butter, egg, kosher salt, and remaining ¼ cup sugar, beating until combined, about 2 minutes. Switch to the dough hook attachment. Add 3 cups flour, and beat for 2 minutes. Add remaining 1 cup flour, and beat until combined and dough pulls away from sides of bowl, about 1 minute.

3. Turn out dough onto a lightly floured surface, and knead until smooth and elastic, 4 to 5 times. Spray a large bowl with cooking spray. Place dough in bowl, turning to grease top. Cover and let rise in a warm, draft-free place (75°) until doubled in size, 1 hour to 1 hour and 30 minutes.

4. Spray 2 (12-cup) muffin pans with cooking spray.

5. Turn out dough onto a lightly floured surface, and divide in half. Divide each half into 36 pieces; shape pieces into balls. Place 3 balls in each prepared muffin cup. Brush tops with remaining 2 tablespoons melted butter. Sprinkle 12 rolls with sea salt, and sprinkle 12 rolls with poppy seeds. Cover and let stand in a warm, draft-free place (75°) until puffed, about 30 minutes.

6. Preheat oven to 375°.

7. Bake until golden brown, 15 to 20 minutes. Serve warm.

CHEESY GARLIC SKILLET ROLLS

MAKES ABOUT 24

These skillet rolls are packed with pockets of melty mozzarella and glistening with garlic-herb butter.

4 cups all-purpose flour
2¼ teaspoons instant yeast
2¼ teaspoons kosher salt, divided
1½ teaspoons sugar
1¼ cups warm water (120° to 125°)
⅓ cup olive oil
8 low-moisture part-skim mozzarella string cheese sticks*
½ cup grated Parmesan cheese
¼ cup unsalted butter, melted
1 tablespoon finely chopped fresh parsley
1 teaspoon Italian seasoning
1 teaspoon garlic powder

1. In the bowl of a stand mixer fitted with the dough hook attachment, combine flour, yeast, 2 teaspoons salt, and sugar. With mixer on low speed, gradually add 1¼ cups warm water and oil, beating until combined. Increase mixer speed to medium, and beat until smooth and elastic, 7 to 10 minutes. Spray a large bowl with cooking spray. Place dough in bowl, turning to grease top. Cover with plastic wrap, and let rise in a warm, draft-free place (75°) until doubled in size, about 1 hour.
2. Preheat oven to 400°. Spray a 10-inch cast-iron skillet with cooking spray.
3. Cut mozzarella sticks into 24 (¾-inch) pieces and remaining mozzarella into ⅜-inch pieces.
4. Turn out dough onto a lightly floured surface. Roll dough to ½-inch thickness. Using a 2-inch round cutter, cut dough into 24 rounds, rerolling scraps as necessary. Place 1 (¾-inch) piece mozzarella in center of each round. Wrap dough around cheese, pinching seam to seal. Place in prepared skillet, seam side down. Place ⅜-inch pieces mozzarella between rolls in skillet. Scatter any remaining mozzarella cheese over rolls.
5. Bake for 15 minutes. Sprinkle with Parmesan. Bake 5 minutes more.
6. In a small bowl, stir together melted butter, parsley, Italian seasoning, garlic powder, and remaining ¼ teaspoon salt. Brush rolls with butter mixture. Serve immediately.

We used Kraft String Cheese.

ENGLISH MUFFIN LOAVES

MAKES 2 (8½X4½-INCH) LOAVES

Nooks, crannies, and everything else to love about English muffins await in these two toaster-ready loaves.

- **6¼ cups all-purpose flour, divided**
- **2 (0.25-ounce) packages active dry yeast**
- **5 teaspoons kosher salt**
- **2½ teaspoons sugar**
- **¼ teaspoon baking soda**
- **2 cups warm whole milk (120° to 130°)**
- **⅔ cup warm water (120° to 130°)**
- **2 tablespoons vegetable oil**
- **2 tablespoons plain yellow cornmeal, divided**
- **1 large egg, beaten**

1. In the bowl of a stand mixer fitted with the paddle attachment, whisk together 6 cups flour, yeast, salt, sugar, and baking soda.

2. Add warm milk, ⅔ cup warm water, and oil to flour mixture. Beat at medium-low speed until a shaggy dough forms, stopping to scrape paddle and sides of bowl, 1 to 2 minutes. (Mixture will be shaggy, but no dry bits of flour should remain.)

3. Switch to the dough hook attachment. Beat at low speed until a soft, slightly sticky dough forms, stopping to scrape dough hook and sides of bowl, 13 to 15 minutes. Beat in remaining ¼ cup flour, 1 tablespoon at a time, if dough is too sticky. Turn out dough onto a lightly floured surface, and shape into a smooth round.

4. Spray a large bowl with cooking spray. Place dough in bowl, turning to grease top. Cover and let rise in a warm, draft-free place (75°) until doubled in size, 30 to 45 minutes.

5. Spray 2 (8½x4½-inch) cast-iron loaf pans with cooking spray. Line pans with parchment paper, letting excess extend over sides of pans. Lightly spray parchment; sprinkle 1 tablespoon cornmeal into bottom and up sides of each pan.

6. Turn out dough onto a lightly floured surface, and divide in half. Lightly pat one portion of dough into an 8½x6-inch rectangle. Working with one long side closest to you, fold top third of dough to center, pressing to seal. Fold bottom third over to center, pressing to seal. Fold dough in half lengthwise so long sides meet. Using the heel of your hand, firmly press edges to seal. Shape dough into an 8½-inch-long rectangle with even thickness. Place, seam side down, in prepared pan. Repeat with remaining dough and prepared pan. Loosely cover pans, and let rise in a warm, draft-free place (75°) until puffed, 15 to 20 minutes.

7. Preheat oven to 400°.

8. Lightly brush egg onto loaves; sprinkle remaining 1 tablespoon cornmeal onto loaves.

9. Bake until top is golden brown and dry, 20 to 25 minutes. Loosely cover loaves with foil and bake until an instant-read thermometer inserted in center of loaves registers 190°, 5 to 10 minutes more. Let cool in pans on wire racks for 10 minutes. Using excess parchment as handles, remove from pans, and let cool on wire racks for 30 minutes before serving.

KITCHEN TIP Tightly wrap cooled loaves in plastic wrap, and freeze for up to 1 month. Let them thaw overnight in the refrigerator before serving.

SAGE PECAN PESTO

MAKES ABOUT 1 CUP

While traditional pesto calls for basil and pine nuts, our take utilizes argula, sage, and pecans for a robust sauce. Twirl it into pasta, dollop it onto toasted bread, and spread it onto pizza crust.

- **⅓ cup pecan halves**
- **3 cups firmly packed fresh arugula**
- **½ cup lightly packed fresh parsley leaves**
- **⅓ cup lightly packed fresh sage leaves**
- **⅓ cup grated Parmesan cheese**
- **1 clove garlic**
- **½ teaspoon kosher salt**
- **¼ teaspoon ground black pepper**
- **½ teaspoon lemon zest**
- **⅓ cup plus 2 tablespoons extra-virgin olive oil**
- **1 tablespoon fresh lemon juice**

1. In a 10-inch cast-iron skillet, cook pecans over medium-high heat, stirring frequently, until fragrant and lightly browned, about 5 minutes. Remove from pan and set aside to let cool.

2. Fill same skillet with water; bring to a boil over medium-high heat. Add arugula, parsley, and sage; cook, stirring occasionally, until bright green and wilted, 30 seconds to 1 minute. Using a slotted spoon, transfer greens to an ice water bath; let cool. Drain greens well; thoroughly squeeze dry (See Kitchen Tip).

3. In the work bowl of a food processor, add toasted pecans, Parmesan, garlic, salt, pepper, and lemon zest; pulse until coarsely chopped, stopping to scrape sides of bowl. Add greens; pulse until coarsely chopped. Add oil and lemon juice, processing until well combined, stopping to scrape bowl. Refrigerate in an airtight container for up to 1 week.

KITCHEN TIP Blanching the arugula and herbs sets their vivid green color and helps prevent the pesto from turning dark.

ROASTED BERRY-MISO HUMMUS

MAKES ABOUT 2 CUPS

Fermented soybeans add an earthy, salty flavor that balances the tangy sweetness from the roasted summer berries.

- ½ cup fresh cherries, pitted and halved
- ½ cup fresh strawberries, quartered
- ½ cup fresh blackberries, sliced
- 4 tablespoons fresh lemon juice, divided
- ½ cup plus 2 tablespoons olive oil, divided
- ¾ teaspoon kosher salt, divided
- 2 cups canned or cooked chickpeas, drained and rinsed (see Kitchen Tip)
- 2 tablespoons tahini
- 2 tablespoons white miso paste
- 1 lemon, zested
- ⅛ teaspoon crushed red pepper

Garnish: crushed red pepper, lemon zest

1. Preheat oven to 425°.
2. In an 8-inch square baking dish, stir together cherries, strawberries, blackberries, 2 tablespoons lemon juice, 1 tablespoon oil, and ¼ teaspoon salt. Bake until tender, about 20 minutes. Let cool to room temperature.
3. In the work bowl of a food processor, place chickpeas; process until chickpeas resemble coarse meal. Add tahini, miso paste, lemon zest, red pepper, remaining 2 tablespoons lemon juice, and remaining ½ teaspoon salt; process until combined. With processor running, add remaining ½ cup plus 1 tablespoon oil in a slow, steady stream until desired consistency is reached, 30 seconds to 1 minute, stopping to scrape sides of bowl. Refrigerate until ready to serve. (Hummus will keep refrigerated for up to 1 week.)
4. To serve, top hummus with roasted berry mixture. Garnish with red pepper and lemon zest, if desired.

KITCHEN TIP Not into canned chickpeas? You can achieve the same product by soaking ½ cup dried chickpeas in water and letting them stand overnight. Drain; place in a medium saucepan with water to cover by 2 inches. Bring to a boil over medium-high heat. Reduce heat to medium; cover and cook until tender, 1 hour to 1 hour and 30 minutes. Drain, and let cool completely.

CLASSIC GUACAMOLE

MAKES 1¼ CUPS

We've given you all the tools you'll need to create this addicting crowd favorite, and even some new ways to flavor it that will keep you coming back for more.

- **2 large ripe avocados, halved and pitted**
- **2 tablespoons minced red onion, rinsed**
- **1 tablespoon chopped fresh cilantro**
- **2 teaspoons fresh lime juice**
- **½ teaspoon kosher salt**
- **½ teaspoon minced garlic**
- **Garnish: chopped fresh cilantro**
- **Tortilla chips, to serve**

FOR GUACAMOLE

1. Scoop avocado pulp into a large bowl. Using a potato masher or fork, mash avocado to desired consistency. Gently stir in onion, cilantro, lime juice, salt, and garlic. Garnish with cilantro, if desired. Serve with tortilla chips.

FOR BACON AND COTIJA GUACAMOLE

1. Using Classic Guacamole as the base, stir in 4 slices cooked and crumbled bacon and 2 tablespoons crumbled Cotija cheese. Garnish with additional cooked and crumbled bacon and crumbled Cotija cheese, if desired.

FOR MARGARITA GUACAMOLE

1. Using Classic Guacamole as the base, stir in 1 tablespoon fresh orange juice and 1 teaspoon silver tequila. Garnish with orange zest and flaked sea salt, if desired.

KITCHEN TIP Place minced red onion in a bowl of cold water for about 10 minutes, drain. This will take out some of the bite.

SPINACH ARTICHOKE DIP

MAKES ABOUT 6 CUPS

This crowd-pleasing snack is a one-skillet wonder that's every bit as creamy and cheesy as you'd expect, but it also has a welcomed and unexpected crunch thanks to the addition of water chestnuts.

- ¼ cup unsalted butter
- ½ cup chopped sweet onion
- 2 cloves garlic, chopped
- ¼ cup all-purpose flour
- 2 cups heavy whipping cream
- 1 cup shredded low-moisture part-skim mozzarella cheese
- ¾ cup freshly grated Parmesan cheese, divided
- 1 (9-ounce) bag fresh spinach, chopped
- 1 (14-ounce) can artichoke hearts, drained and chopped
- 1 (8-ounce) can sliced water chestnuts, drained and chopped
- 1 teaspoon hot sauce
- 1 teaspoon kosher salt
- ⅛ teaspoon crushed red pepper
- Toasted French bread slices, to serve

1. Preheat oven to 450°.

2. In a 10-inch cast-iron skillet, melt butter over medium heat. Add onion and garlic; cook, stirring occasionally, until softened, 3 to 5 minutes. Whisk in flour until smooth; cook, whisking constantly, for 2 minutes. Gradually whisk in cream until thick and smooth. Whisk in mozzarella and ½ cup Parmesan until melted and smooth.

3. Stir in spinach in batches until wilted. Stir in artichokes, water chestnuts, hot sauce, and salt until well combined. Sprinkle with remaining ¼ cup Parmesan and red pepper.

4. Bake until golden brown and bubbly, 10 to 12 minutes. Let stand for 10 minutes. Serve with bread.

QUESO FUNDIDO

MAKES 10 TO 12 SERVINGS

Crumbled chorizo and fresh jalapeño pepper infuse this dip with a spicy kick.

- ½ pound fresh Mexican chorizo, casings removed
- 1 small yellow onion, chopped
- 1 small jalapeño, seeded and diced
- 2 cloves garlic, minced
- 3 cups shredded Monterey Jack cheese
- Miniature bell peppers, to serve
- Garnish: diced plum tomatoes, chopped fresh cilantro, diced jalapeño

1. Preheat oven to 350°.
2. In an 8-inch cast-iron skillet, combine chorizo, onion, and jalapeño; cook over medium heat, using the back of a spoon to break up chorizo, until chorizo is crumbled and vegetables are tender, about 5 minutes. Add garlic; cook until fragrant, about 1 minute. Reserve 2 tablespoons chorizo mixture for garnish. Sprinkle cheese over remaining chorizo mixture. Do not stir.
3. Bake until cheese is bubbly, 12 to 15 minutes. Serve with bell peppers. Garnish with reserved chorizo mixture, tomatoes, cilantro, and jalapeño, if desired.

BEER CHEESE DIP

MAKES ABOUT 8 SERVINGS

No party will be complete without this smoky, cheesy dip. Pair with pretzel bites for the ultimate party experience.

- ½ pound smoked sausage,* cut into 3-inch strips
- 2 tablespoons unsalted butter
- ¼ cup all-purpose flour
- ½ cup heavy whipping cream
- 1 (12-ounce) bottle beer
- 2 cups shredded sharp Cheddar cheese
- 1 teaspoon smoked paprika, plus more to taste
- 1 teaspoon stone-ground mustard
- 1 teaspoon hot sauce
- ½ teaspoon garlic powder
- ¼ teaspoon kosher salt
- Pretzel bites, to serve
- Garnish: sliced green onion, crushed red pepper

1. In a 10-inch cast-iron skillet, cook sausage over medium-low heat, stirring frequently, until lightly browned and cooked through, 15 to 20 minutes. Remove from skillet using a slotted spoon. Let drain on paper towels; reserve 2 tablespoons drippings in skillet.

2. Add butter to drippings in skillet; cook over medium-low heat until butter is melted. Whisk in flour. Cook, whisking constantly, for 30 seconds. Slowly whisk in cream; slowly whisk in beer. Cook, whisking constantly, until thickened, smooth, and bubbly, about 8 minutes.

3. Remove skillet from heat. Gradually add cheese, stirring until smooth. Stir in paprika, mustard, hot sauce, garlic powder, and salt. Season with paprika. Serve immediately with sausage and pretzel bites. Garnish with green onion and red pepper, if desired.

**We used Conecuh Smoked Sausage.*

LEMON BAKED FETA

MAKES 6 SERVINGS

When life hands you lemons, make this irresistible dish.

- 1 (16-ounce) package creamy feta cheese packed in brine, drained
- 4 tablespoons olive oil, divided
- 2 teaspoons Cajun seasoning
- 2 tablespoons chopped preserved lemon
- 6 to 8 (¼-inch-thick) slices lemon, divided
- 1 (8-ounce) container assorted cherry tomatoes
- ¼ cup seedless kalamata olives
- ¼ cup seedless Castelvetrano olives
- 4 (4-inch) pieces lemon peel
- 2 tablespoons fresh lemon juice
- 3 sprigs fresh thyme
- 3 sprigs fresh rosemary
- Toasted baguette slices, to serve
- Garnish: fresh rosemary

1. Preheat oven to 400°.

2. In a 9-inch square baking dish or a 9-inch ovenproof skillet, place feta in center of pan. Drizzle feta with 1 tablespoon oil and sprinkle with Cajun seasoning. Top feta with preserved lemon and 4 lemon slices.

3. In a medium bowl, toss together tomatoes, all olives, lemon peel, lemon juice, and remaining 3 tablespoons oil. Pour tomato mixture around feta. Arrange thyme, rosemary, and remaining 2 to 4 lemon slices on top of tomato mixture.

4. Bake until feta is slightly melted and light golden brown and tomatoes are cooked, about 20 minutes. Discard rosemary and thyme. Serve with bread. Garnish with rosemary, if desired.

POTATO CHIPS

MAKES 8 TO 10 SERVINGS

These addictively crunchy home-fried chips will satisfy all your salty cravings.

FOR POTATO CHIPS

- 4 large russet potatoes, sliced ⅛ inch thick
- ¾ cup distilled white vinegar
- Canola oil, for frying
- 1 teaspoon kosher salt or desired seasoning blend (recipes follow)

FOR BARBECUE SEASONING

- 2 tablespoons smoked paprika
- 2 tablespoons firmly packed brown sugar
- 4 teaspoons onion powder
- 2 teaspoons kosher salt
- 2 teaspoons garlic powder
- 1 teaspoon chili powder

FOR CHILI-LIME SEASONING

- 1 lime, zested
- 2 tablespoons sugar
- 4 teaspoons ground cumin
- 2 teaspoons kosher salt
- 2 teaspoons chili powder
- 1 teaspoon ground red pepper
- ½ teaspoon crushed red pepper

FOR POTATO CHIPS

1. Rinse and drain potatoes; repeat until water is clear, 3 to 4 times. In a large bowl, soak potatoes in vinegar and water to cover for at least 30 minutes or up to 2 hours. Drain; pat dry.

2. In a large Dutch oven, pour oil to a depth of 4 inches, and heat over medium heat until a deep-fry thermometer registers 300°. Working in batches, fry potatoes, stirring frequently, until golden brown and crispy, 6 to 8 minutes.

3. Place chips on a large rimmed baking sheet; sprinkle with salt or desired seasoning blend.

FOR BARBECUE SEASONING

1. In a small bowl, stir together all ingredients.

FOR CHILI-LIME SEASONING

1. In a small bowl, stir together all ingredients.

TIPS FOR CRISPY CHIPS Rinse the potato slices to remove excess starch, ensuring the crispiest chip. Soak the slices in vinegar water to control the breakdown of pectin in the potato. This creates a sturdier chip that is less likely to crumble. Stir the chips during the frying process to prevent the chips from sticking together and to help them cook more evenly.

CITRUS-ROSEMARY SHRIMP ON THE ROCKS

MAKES 6 TO 8 SERVINGS

Roasting on a bed of seasoned rock salt and citrus infuses the shrimp with bright and briny flavor.

- 3 pounds rock salt
- 2 tablespoons whole black peppercorns
- 1 tablespoon whole coriander seeds
- Fresh rosemary sprigs
- 6 heads garlic, halved
- 1 pound whole head-on fresh shrimp
- 1 lime, cut into wedges
- ½ grapefruit, cut into wedges
- Garnish: fresh rosemary sprigs

1. Preheat oven to 475°.
2. In a large bowl, stir together rock salt, peppercorns, coriander, rosemary, and garlic. Place half of salt mixture in a 12-inch cast-iron skillet.
3. Bake for 10 minutes. Carefully remove from oven. Add shrimp, lime, and grapefruit; cover with remaining salt mixture. Bake until shrimp are fully cooked, about 10 minutes more. Garnish with rosemary, if desired.

BAKED OYSTERS

MAKES 18

If serving a crowd, use shucked oysters with metal or ceramic oyster shell dishes.

- ¼ cup unsalted butter, softened
- 1 clove garlic, minced
- 1 teaspoon minced fresh parsley
- ½ teaspoon lemon zest
- ½ teaspoon minced fresh thyme
- ½ teaspoon hot sauce
- ⅛ teaspoon kosher salt
- ⅛ teaspoon ground black pepper
- 6 tablespoons panko (Japanese bread crumbs)
- 2 tablespoons grated Parmesan cheese
- 18 fresh oysters on half shell
- Lemon wedges, to serve
- Garnish: chopped fresh parsley

1. Preheat oven to 450°.
2. In a small bowl, stir together butter, garlic, parsley, lemon zest, thyme, hot sauce, salt, and pepper until well combined.
3. In another small bowl, combine bread crumbs and cheese.
4. In a 13x9-inch baking dish or on a large rimmed baking sheet, place oysters on half shell.
5. Bake for 3 minutes. Evenly divide butter mixture among oysters; sprinkle with bread crumb mixture.
6. Bake until edges of oysters curl and bread crumbs are golden brown, about 5 minutes more. Serve immediately with lemon wedges. Garnish with parsley, if desired.

SOUPS AND SALADS

chapter 2

BUTTERNUT SQUASH AND BACON SOUP

MAKES 6 TO 8 SERVINGS

A swirl of sour cream and a sprinkling of crumbled bacon pack this velvety soup with welcome richness.

- ¼ cup unsalted butter
- 1 cup chopped peeled carrot
- 1 cup chopped celery
- 1 cup chopped sweet onion
- ⅓ cup thinly sliced green onion tops
- 1 clove garlic, minced
- ¼ cup all-purpose flour
- 3¾ pounds butternut squash, peeled and cut into 1-inch cubes
- 6 cups vegetable broth
- 1 tablespoon minced fresh rosemary
- 1½ teaspoons kosher salt
- ¾ teaspoon ground black pepper, divided
- 1 cup sour cream
- ½ pound thick-cut bacon, cooked and chopped

Garnish: fresh rosemary

1. In a large Dutch oven, melt butter over medium heat. Add carrot, celery, sweet onion, green onion, and garlic; cook until the onion starts to soften, 4 to 5 minutes. Add flour; cook for 2 minutes, stirring constantly. Add squash, broth, rosemary, salt, and ½ teaspoon pepper; bring to a boil over medium-high heat. Reduce heat to low; simmer until squash is tender, about 10 minutes.

2. Working in batches, transfer soup to the container of a blender. Secure lid, and remove center piece of lid to let steam escape. Place a clean towel over opening in lid to avoid splatters, and process until smooth.

3. In a medium bowl, whisk together sour cream and remaining ¼ teaspoon pepper.

4. Divide soup among serving bowls. Spoon sour cream mixture in center of each bowl, and swirl using the tip of a knife. Top with crumbled bacon. Garnish with rosemary, if desired.

APPLE AND BEER CHEESE SOUP

MAKES 6 SERVINGS

This cozy soup has complex flavor thanks to tart apple, sweet onion, and IPA beer.

- 5 tablespoons salted butter, divided
- 1 cup chopped sweet onion
- ½ cup chopped carrot
- 1½ cups chopped peeled Granny Smith apple
- ½ teaspoon kosher salt
- ½ teaspoon ground black pepper
- ¼ teaspoon dry mustard
- ¼ teaspoon ground red pepper
- 1 clove garlic, minced
- ¼ cup all-purpose flour
- 1 (12-ounce) bottle IPA beer
- 1 cup chicken stock
- 1 cup whole milk
- 6 ounces shredded sharp Cheddar cheese
- 4 ounces shredded smoked Gouda cheese
- 1 cup cubed marbled rye bread
- ½ cup chopped pecans, toasted

1. In a large Dutch oven, melt 3 tablespoons butter over medium heat. Add onion, carrot, apple, salt, and black pepper; cook until mixture becomes tender, about 5 minutes. Add dry mustard, red pepper, and garlic; cook, stirring often, until mixture is very tender, about 3 minutes. Add flour; cook, stirring constantly, for 3 minutes.

2. Reduce heat to medium-low. Slowly add beer, stock, and milk, stirring constantly. Increase heat to medium-high. Bring to a boil, stirring constantly, until thickened, about 3 minutes. Remove from heat; let stand for 3 minutes.

3. Working in batches, transfer soup to the container of a blender. Secure lid on blender and remove center piece of lid to let steam escape. Place a clean towel over opening in lid to avoid splatters, and process until very smooth. Return mixture to Dutch oven and heat over medium-low. Working in batches, add cheeses, stirring until melted.

4. In a small skillet, melt remaining 2 tablespoons butter over medium-high heat. Add bread, stirring constantly, until toasted, about 5 minutes. Top each serving with croutons and pecans.

PECAN SOUP

MAKES 4 TO 6 SERVINGS

The delicious taste of pecans shines in this comforting soup, which is similar to chestnut soup.

- ½ cup unsalted butter
- 1 cup chopped leek, white and light green parts only (about 1 leek)
- ½ cup chopped shallot (about 1 large shallot)
- ½ cup chopped celery
- ½ cup chopped peeled carrot (about 1 large carrot)
- 1 tablespoon chopped garlic
- 1 tablespoon kosher salt
- ½ teaspoon ground black pepper
- ¼ teaspoon ground red pepper
- 1 pound pecan pieces
- 4 cups vegetable broth
- 3 cups heavy whipping cream
- Garnish: toasted pecans, crème fraîche, sliced fresh chives

1. In a large Dutch oven, melt butter over medium heat. Add leek, shallot, celery, carrot, garlic, salt, black pepper, and red pepper; cook until vegetables are tender, about 10 minutes. Increase heat to medium-high. Add pecans, broth, and cream; bring to a boil. Reduce heat to medium, and simmer until pecans are plumped and liquid is slightly thickened, 20 to 25 minutes.

2. Transfer half of soup to the container of a blender. Secure lid on blender, and remove center piece of lid to let steam escape; place a clean towel over opening in lid to avoid splatters. Process until smooth. Transfer to a bowl. Repeat with remaining soup. Return soup to pot, and keep warm until ready to serve. Garnish with toasted pecans, crème fraîche, and chives, if desired.

SWEET POTATO AND LENTIL SOUP

MAKES 8 SERVINGS

This satisfying dish is our new favorite version of vegetable soup. It's so filling your family will never notice it's meatless!

- 8 cups vegetable stock
- 1½ cups dried brown lentils
- 1 cup chopped sweet onion
- ½ cup chopped carrot
- ½ cup chopped celery
- 2 small sweet potatoes (1¼ pounds), peeled and cut into 1-inch cubes
- 3 cloves garlic, minced
- 1 (15-ounce) can diced tomatoes
- 1 tablespoon chopped fresh rosemary
- 1 teaspoon dried thyme leaves
- 2 teaspoons kosher salt
- 1 teaspoon ground black pepper
- 2 bay leaves
- 3 cups chopped fresh collard greens

1. In a 6-quart slow cooker, combine stock, lentils, onion, carrot, celery, sweet potatoes, garlic, tomatoes, rosemary, thyme, salt, pepper, and bay leaves. Cover and cook on low for 4 hours.

2. Stir in collard greens. Continue to cook until wilted, about 30 minutes.

COCONUT SQUASH SOUP

MAKES 6 TO 8 SERVINGS

The mild earthiness of butternut squash and nutty acorn squash pairs with creamy coconut for a flavorful dish you'll want to curl up with during cold nights.

- 2 tablespoons olive oil
- 2 (1½-pound) acorn squash, seeded and cut into 1-inch cubes (about 6 cups)
- 1 (3½-pound) butternut squash, peeled, seeded, and cut into 1-inch cubes (about 4 cups)
- 1 medium onion, chopped
- 3 medium carrots, peeled and chopped
- 3 cloves garlic, minced
- 2 teaspoons kosher salt
- ½ teaspoon ground black pepper
- 4 cups vegetable broth
- 1 (15-ounce) can unsweetened coconut milk
- 2 teaspoons poultry seasoning
- 4 cups torn fresh collard greens
- 1 (15-ounce) can chickpeas, rinsed and drained
- 1½ tablespoons apple cider vinegar
- Sour cream, crushed red pepper, and bread, to serve

1. In a large Dutch oven, heat oil over medium heat. Add all squash and onion; cook, stirring frequently, until squash and onion are tender, 25 to 30 minutes.

2. Add carrot, garlic, salt, and black pepper to squash mixture; cook, stirring occasionally, for 5 minutes. Add broth, coconut milk, and poultry seasoning. Bring to a boil over medium heat; reduce heat, and simmer, stirring occasionally, for 30 minutes.

3. Add collards, chickpeas, and vinegar to soup, stirring to combine. Cook until heated through, about 5 minutes. Serve with sour cream, red pepper, and bread.

SMOKY TOMATO SOUP

MAKES 6 TO 8 SERVINGS

A smoky twist on traditional tomato soup, this dish adds the spicy punch of chipotle and chili powder for a delicious meal.

FOR SOUP
- ¼ cup olive oil
- 1½ cups chopped onion
- 1½ tablespoons minced garlic
- ¼ cup all-purpose flour
- 1 (32-ounce) container chicken stock
- 1 (28-ounce) can fire-roasted crushed tomatoes, undrained
- ½ teaspoon ground chipotle chile pepper
- ¼ teaspoon chili powder
- 1 teaspoon kosher salt
- ½ teaspoon ground black pepper
- 1½ tablespoons thinly sliced fresh basil
- Bacon Cheese Straws (recipe follows), to serve
- Garnish: thinly sliced fresh basil, ground black pepper

FOR BACON CHEESE STRAWS
- 6 slices bacon, chopped
- 1¼ cups all-purpose flour
- ½ teaspoon kosher salt
- ¼ teaspoon garlic powder
- ¼ teaspoon dry mustard
- ¼ teaspoon smoked paprika
- ¼ teaspoon ground black pepper
- 1 cup shredded Havarti cheese, room temperature
- 6 tablespoons unsalted butter, softened

FOR SOUP

1. In a large Dutch oven, heat oil over medium-high heat. Add onion and garlic; cook, stirring occasionally, until tender, 3 to 5 minutes.

2. Stir in flour until well combined; cook 2 to 3 minutes. Gradually stir in half of stock. Bring to a low boil; cook until thickened, stirring frequently. Stir in remaining stock, tomatoes, ground chipotle chile pepper, chili powder, salt, and black pepper; bring just to a boil. Reduce heat to medium-low; simmer, uncovered, stirring occasionally, until thickened, 20 to 30 minutes.

3. Transfer half of soup to the container of a blender. Secure lid on blender and remove center piece of lid to let steam escape. Place a clean towel over opening in lid to avoid splatters, and process until smooth. Return blended soup to soup mixture in pot.

4. Add basil, and stir to combine. Serve immediately with Bacon Cheese Straws. Garnish with basil and black pepper, if desired.

FOR BACON CHEESE STRAWS

1. Preheat oven to 400°.

2. In a large skillet, cook bacon over medium heat until crisp. Remove bacon; let drain on paper towels.

3. In the work bowl of a food processor, combine flour, salt, garlic powder, mustard, paprika, and pepper; pulse 2 to 4 times until well combined. Add chopped bacon, cheese, and butter. Pulse until a dough forms.

4. Spoon dough into a piping bag fitted with a Wilton 4B open star tip. Pipe dough into 6-inch lines, spaced about 1 inch apart on unlined, ungreased baking sheets (see Kitchen Tip).

5. Bake until lightly golden and crisp, 8 to 10 minutes.

KITCHEN TIP Bake on unlined, ungreased baking sheets to ensure the cheese straws are crisp.

TOMATO BEEF ROAST WITH CORNMEAL-THYME DUMPLINGS

MAKES 4 TO 6 SERVINGS

This hearty twist on chicken and dumplings is all of our favorite comfort foods in one dish.

- 1 tablespoon olive oil
- 1 (2½-pound) chuck roast
- 2¼ teaspoons kosher salt, divided
- 1 teaspoon ground black pepper
- 4 cloves garlic, smashed
- 1 (28-ounce) can whole peeled tomatoes, undrained
- ¼ cup dried porcini mushrooms
- 4 sprigs fresh thyme
- ⅔ cup all-purpose flour
- ⅓ cup plain yellow cornmeal
- 1 tablespoon chopped fresh thyme
- 2 teaspoons firmly packed light brown sugar
- 1 teaspoon baking powder
- 1 tablespoon cold unsalted butter, cubed
- ½ cup whole milk
- Garnish: chopped fresh thyme, ground black pepper

1. Preheat oven to 275°.

2. In a large enameled cast-iron Dutch oven, heat oil over medium-high heat. Sprinkle roast with 2 teaspoons salt and pepper. Add roast to Dutch oven; sear, turning occasionally, until browned on all sides, about 3 minutes per side. Remove from Dutch oven. Add garlic, tomatoes, and mushrooms, scraping bottom of pan and using the back of a spoon to crush tomatoes; bring to a boil. Remove from heat. Add roast and thyme sprigs; cover.

3. Bake until fork tender, about 2 hours and 30 minutes. Let stand for 5 minutes; using 2 forks, shred roast.

4. In a medium bowl, stir together flour, cornmeal, chopped thyme, brown sugar, baking powder, and remaining ¼ teaspoon salt. Using a pastry blender, cut in cold butter until mixture is crumbly. Stir in milk until combined; let stand for 5 minutes. Drop mixture by tablespoonfuls on top of roast. Cover and cook over medium-low heat until a wooden pick inserted in center of dumplings comes out clean, about 20 minutes. Garnish with thyme and pepper, if desired.

CHICKEN AND SWEET POTATO DROP DUMPLINGS

MAKES 8 TO 10 SERVINGS

They say chicken soup is good for the soul, and our updated take on chicken and dumplings is the embodiment of this universal truth.

FOR SOUP
- 2 tablespoons unsalted butter
- 2 cups chopped onion
- 1½ cups coarsely chopped carrot
- ½ cup coarsely chopped celery
- 6 cups chicken broth, divided
- 1 tablespoon chopped fresh sage
- 1 tablespoon chopped fresh thyme
- 1 tablespoon fresh lemon juice
- 1 teaspoon kosher salt
- ½ teaspoon ground black pepper, plus more to taste
- ½ teaspoon garlic powder
- ⅓ cup all-purpose flour
- 3 cups chopped cooked chicken

FOR DUMPLINGS
- 1½ cups all-purpose flour
- 1 teaspoon baking powder
- ¾ teaspoon kosher salt
- ⅛ teaspoon ground black pepper
- ½ cup coarsely mashed cooked peeled sweet potato
- ½ cup whole buttermilk
- 1 tablespoon unsalted butter, melted
- 1 large egg, lightly beaten

Garnish: fresh thyme, fresh sage

FOR SOUP

1. In a 5-quart cast-iron Dutch oven, melt butter over medium-high heat. Add onion, carrot, and celery; cook until lightly browned, about 4 minutes. Stir in 5½ cups broth, sage, thyme, lemon juice, salt, pepper, and garlic powder; bring to a boil. Reduce heat to medium-low; cover and cook until vegetables are crisp-tender, about 8 minutes.

2. In a small bowl, whisk together flour and remaining ½ cup broth; stir into pot. Cook, stirring occasionally, until slightly thickened, 6 to 8 minutes. Stir in chicken.

FOR DUMPLINGS

1. In a large bowl, whisk together flour, baking powder, salt, and pepper. In a small bowl, whisk together sweet potato, buttermilk, melted butter, and egg. Stir sweet potato mixture into flour mixture until a dough forms. (Dough will be soft.) With floured hands, roll dough into 12 balls.

2. Bring soup to a boil over medium-high heat; quickly but carefully drop dough balls into soup. Reduce heat to medium-low; cover and cook, without stirring, until dumplings are puffed and cooked through, 15 to 17 minutes. Season with additional pepper. Garnish with thyme and sage, if desired.

CHICKEN AND DUMPLINGS

MAKES 6 TO 8 SERVINGS

This classic meal is the ultimate Southern meal done right.

- 2 tablespoons vegetable oil
- 4 large carrots, peeled and chopped (about 2 cups)
- 3 stalks celery, chopped
- 1 medium yellow onion, chopped
- 4 cloves garlic, minced
- 3 tablespoons salted butter
- ⅓ cup all-purpose flour
- 2 (32-ounce) containers less-sodium chicken broth
- 1 tablespoon plus 1 teaspoon kosher salt, divided
- ½ teaspoon ground black pepper
- 4 cups shredded rotisserie chicken
- 1 cup half-and-half
- 1 tablespoon plus 1 teaspoon chopped fresh thyme, divided
- 1 tablespoon chopped fresh dill
- 2 cups self-rising flour, plus more for dusting
- 3 tablespoons cold salted butter, cubed
- ½ cup whole milk
- 1 tablespoon chopped fresh parsley
- Garnish: fresh thyme, ground black pepper

1. In a large enamel-coated cast-iron Dutch oven, heat oil over medium heat. Add carrot, celery, and onion. Cook, stirring frequently, until vegetables are tender, about 5 minutes.

2. Add garlic to vegetable mixture; cook, stirring constantly, for 1 minute. Add butter; cook, stirring constantly, until butter is melted. Add all-purpose flour; cook, stirring constantly, for 2 minutes. Add broth, 1 tablespoon salt, and pepper. Cook, stirring occasionally, until slightly thickened, about 30 minutes.

3. Add chicken and half-and-half to soup; bring to a boil over medium heat, stirring occasionally. Reduce heat to low. Stir in 1 tablespoon thyme and dill.

4. In a medium bowl, whisk together self-rising flour and remaining 1 teaspoon salt. Using a pastry blender, cut in cold butter until mixture is crumbly. Stir in milk, parsley, and remaining 1 teaspoon thyme just until dry ingredients are moistened.

5. Lightly dust work surface with self-rising flour; turn out dough onto prepared surface. Knead until dough comes together, 3 to 4 times. Roll dough to ⅛-inch thickness. Using a pizza cutter, cut dough into 1½-inch squares.

6. Drop dumplings, a few at a time, into hot soup. (Do not stir.) Cover and gently shake pot in a circular motion; cook over medium-low heat until dumplings float and are cooked through the center, 4 to 6 minutes. Garnish with thyme and pepper, if desired.

SHRIMP AND OYSTER GUMBO

MAKES ABOUT 8 SERVINGS

Seafood and sausage come together in the tastiest way in this too-good-to-be-true gumbo.

- ½ cup all-purpose flour
- ½ cup vegetable oil
- 1 pound smoked sausage,* cut into ¼-inch slices
- 1½ cups sliced celery
- 1½ cups chopped onion
- 1 cup chopped red bell pepper
- 3 cloves garlic, minced
- 1½ tablespoons fresh thyme leaves
- ½ teaspoon crushed red pepper
- 1 tablespoon plus 2 teaspoons filé powder, divided
- 6 cups seafood stock
- 2 tablespoons Worcestershire sauce
- 1 bay leaf
- 1 pound peeled and deveined large fresh shrimp (tails on)
- 12 shucked fresh oysters
- ½ teaspoon kosher salt
- ½ cup sliced green onion
- Cooked long-grain rice, to serve
- Garnish: sliced green onion

1. In a large cast-iron Dutch oven, combine flour and oil, stirring until smooth. Cook over medium heat until flour mixture turns dark brown in color, stirring constantly, about 10 minutes.

2. Add sausage, celery, onion, bell pepper, garlic, thyme, crushed red pepper, and 1 tablespoon filé powder. Cook until onions are tender, stirring constantly, about 5 minutes. Add stock, Worcestershire, and bay leaf; bring to a boil over high heat. Reduce heat to low and simmer for 1 hour.

3. Stir in remaining 2 teaspoons filé powder and shrimp; simmer for 2 minutes. Add oysters and salt; simmer until oysters are cooked, about 1 minute. Remove bay leaf. Stir in green onion. Serve over rice. Garnish with green onion, if desired.

**We used Conecuh smoked sausage.*

AMBER BEEF STEW

MAKES 4 TO 6 SERVINGS

We used amber lager to add another layer of flavor in this hearty stew.

- 2 tablespoons vegetable oil
- 2 pounds beef chuck roast, cut into 1-inch cubes
- 2 tablespoons unsalted butter
- 2 cups chopped sweet onion (about 1 onion)
- 1 cup chopped celery
- 1 tablespoon chopped fresh thyme
- 1 tablespoon kosher salt
- ½ teaspoon ground black pepper
- ¼ teaspoon crushed red pepper
- ½ teaspoon garlic powder
- 2 tablespoons tomato paste
- 2 tablespoons all-purpose flour
- 1 (12-ounce) bottle amber lager,* room temperature
- 1 (14.5-ounce) can beef broth
- 2 cups (½-inch) chopped peeled sweet potatoes
- Sourdough boule, to serve
- Garnish: chopped fresh parsley, crushed red pepper

1. In a large Dutch oven, heat oil over medium heat. Add half of beef, and cook until browned on all sides, 5 to 7 minutes. Remove beef from pot, and set aside. Repeat with remaining beef.

2. In same pot, melt butter over medium heat. Add onion, celery, thyme, salt, black pepper, red pepper, and garlic powder; cook until onion is softened and translucent. Add tomato paste; cook, stirring frequently, until color deepens, about 3 minutes. Add flour; cook, stirring frequently, until flour is golden brown, 3 to 5 minutes.

3. Increase heat to high, and add beer, scraping browned bits from bottom of pot with a wooden spoon. Bring to a boil, and add beef and broth. Return to a boil, and add sweet potato. Reduce heat to medium, and simmer until meat and sweet potato are tender and liquid has thickened, about 45 minutes. Serve with bread or in a bread bowl. Garnish with parsley and red pepper, if desired.

**We used Abita Amber Lager.*

CUBAN BEEF STEW

MAKES 8 TO 10 SERVINGS

All the flavors of a classic Cuban dish are packed into this comforting stew and made easy by cooking unattended in a slow cooker.

- 2 tablespoons olive oil
- 1 (3½-pound) beef chuck roast
- Kosher salt and ground black pepper, to taste
- ¼ cup dry sherry or white wine
- 1½ (1.41-ounce) boxes sazón seasoning* (6 packets)
- 2 green or red bell peppers, seeded and sliced
- 1 sweet onion, sliced
- 1 (14-ounce) can crushed tomatoes
- 3 tablespoons jarred sofrito*
- 2 cups unsalted beef stock
- 1 (14-ounce) can black-eyed peas, drained
- 1 (6-ounce) can tomato paste
- ½ cup sliced green olives with pimientos
- Plantain chips, thinly sliced red onion, and chopped fresh cilantro, to serve

1. In a large sauté pan, heat oil over medium heat. Lightly sprinkle beef with salt and pepper on all sides. Add beef; cook until browned on all sides, about 4 minutes per side. Transfer beef to a 6-quart slow cooker.

2. Add wine to pan, scraping browned bits from bottom of pan with a wooden spoon. Pour over beef. Sprinkle with sazón seasoning. Add bell pepper, onion, tomatoes, and sofrito. Pour in stock. Cover and cook on high until beef is fork-tender, 5 to 6 hours.

3. Reduce heat to low. Remove beef, and shred with 2 forks. Return beef to slow cooker. Stir in black-eyed peas, tomato paste, and olives (see Kitchen Tip). Season with salt and pepper. Partially cover and cook for 1 hour.

4. Serve immediately, or cover and reduce heat to warm until ready to serve. Serve topped with plantain chips, onion, and cilantro.

**We used Goya Sazón with Coriander & Annatto and Goya Sofrito Tomato Cooking Base.*

KITCHEN TIP To freeze, follow the recipe as directed through step 3, omitting the black-eyed peas and olives; add them to the soup when reheating.

PEANUT AND CHICKEN STEW

MAKES 6 TO 8 SERVINGS

Throughout the world, peanuts often show up in savory dishes, and they're right at home in this sweet and spicy stew.

- **2 tablespoons vegetable oil**
- **8 boneless skinless chicken thighs**
- **1½ teaspoons kosher salt, divided**
- **1 teaspoon ground black pepper**
- **1½ cups chopped onion**
- **1 tablespoon finely chopped peeled fresh ginger**
- **2 cloves garlic, finely chopped**
- **3 cups chicken broth**
- **½ cup creamy peanut butter**
- **3 tablespoons tomato paste**
- **½ teaspoon curry powder**
- **¼ teaspoon ground cumin**
- **¼ teaspoon crushed red pepper**
- **2 cups coarsely chopped peeled sweet potato**
- **1½ cups coarsely chopped peeled parsnip**
- **3 bay leaves**
- **1 tablespoon fresh lime juice**
- **Hot cooked rice, to serve**
- **Garnish: chopped fresh parsley, chopped cocktail peanuts, lime wedges**

1. In a large enameled cast-iron Dutch oven, heat oil over medium-high heat. Reduce heat to medium. Sprinkle chicken with 1 teaspoon salt and black pepper. Add half of chicken to Dutch oven; cook until browned, 2 to 3 minutes per side. Remove from Dutch oven. Repeat with remaining chicken.

2. Add onion to Dutch oven; cook until browned, about 3 minutes. Add ginger and garlic; cook for 1 minute. Add broth, peanut butter, tomato paste, curry powder, cumin, and red pepper, stirring until smooth. Add sweet potato, parsnip, and bay leaves; bring to a simmer, partially cover and cook for 10 minutes.

3. Return chicken to Dutch oven; cook, partially covered, until tender, 35 to 40 minutes. Stir in lime juice and remaining ½ teaspoon salt. Discard bay leaves. Serve over hot cooked rice. Garnish with parsley, peanuts, and lime wedges, if desired.

COCONUT CHILE BEEF TENDERLOIN SALAD

MAKES 4 SERVINGS

You'll be craving salad for dinner once you try these tender beef fillets, perfectly complemented by crunchy haricots verts and a tangy dressing.

FOR SALAD

- 1 tablespoon coconut oil
- 2 Thai bird chiles, minced (see Kitchen Tip)
- 1 tablespoon sugar
- 1 tablespoon soy sauce
- 2 teaspoons lime zest
- 1 teaspoon kosher salt
- 4 beef tenderloin fillets
- 8 ounces haricots verts, blanched
- 4 ounces fresh baby spinach
- Coconut Chile Dressing (recipe follows)

FOR COCONUT CHILE DRESSING

- ½ cup coconut milk
- ¼ cup chopped fresh cilantro
- 2 fresh Thai bird chiles, minced
- 3 tablespoons fresh lime juice
- 1 teaspoon fish sauce

FOR SALAD

1. Preheat oven to 400°.

2. In a large ovenproof skillet, heat oil over medium-high heat. Add chiles, sugar, soy sauce, and zest; cook for 30 seconds. Sprinkle salt over fillets. Add fillets to skillet; cook for 2 minutes per side. Transfer skillet to oven.

3. Bake for 5 minutes. Remove from oven. Cover and let stand for 10 minutes. Thinly slice beef.

4. Divide haricots verts and spinach among 4 serving plates. Top with beef. Drizzle with Coconut Chile Dressing. Serve immediately.

FOR COCONUT CHILE DRESSING

1. In a small bowl, whisk together all ingredients until combined.

KITCHEN TIP Fresh Thai bird chiles can be found at local Asian markets or specialty grocery stores.

GRILLED PERSIMMON AND CRAB SALAD

MAKES 6 TO 8 SERVINGS

Grilling the persimmons amplifies their natural sweetness in this refreshing salad.

- 2 limes, zested
- ½ cup fresh lime juice
- 3 tablespoons honey
- 2 tablespoons grated fresh ginger
- ¾ teaspoon kosher salt
- 2 pounds lump crabmeat, drained and picked free of shell
- 1 Fresno chile pepper, seeded and sliced
- Toasted peanut or sesame oil, for brushing and drizzling
- 4 firm Fuyu persimmons, sliced ¼ inch thick
- ¼ cup chopped fresh basil
- 2 tablespoons chopped fresh mint
- 2 heads fresh baby lettuce
- Garnish: fresh mint

1. In a large bowl, whisk together lime zest and juice, honey, ginger, and salt. Gently stir in crab and chile pepper. Cover and refrigerate for at least 1 hour or until ready to serve.

2. Heat a cast-iron grill pan over medium-high heat. Lightly brush pan with oil. Grill persimmons in batches until lightly browned, about 2 minutes per side. Brush grill pan with oil as needed to prevent sticking. Halve grilled persimmons.

3. Stir basil and mint into crab mixture. Arrange lettuce, crab mixture, and persimmons on a serving platter. Garnish with mint, if desired. Serve immediately.

SPICED LAMB KALE SALAD

MAKES 4 TO 6 SERVINGS

Be sure to serve this with warm toasted flatbread to scoop up bites of lamb mixture.

FOR SALAD

- 1½ pounds coarse ground lamb
- 2 large cloves garlic, finely chopped
- 2 teaspoons Moroccan spice blend
- Kosher salt and ground black pepper, to taste
- 1 large bunch baby carrots, halved lengthwise
- 1 bunch fresh lacinato kale, shredded
- Lemon-Tahini Vinaigrette (recipe follows), divided
- 1 head fresh frisée lettuce, coarsely chopped
- ½ cup fresh parsley leaves
- ½ cup pomegranate arils
- ⅓ cup pine nuts, toasted

FOR LEMON-TAHINI VINAIGRETTE

- ¼ cup finely chopped fresh mint
- 3 tablespoons extra-virgin olive oil
- 3 tablespoons fresh lemon juice
- 2 tablespoons tahini
- 2 tablespoons water
- 1 small shallot, minced
- Kosher salt and ground black pepper, to taste

FOR SALAD

1. Preheat oven to 425°.

2. In a large ovenproof heavy-bottomed skillet, sauté lamb over medium-high heat until crumbly and no pink remains, about 10 minutes. Stir in garlic and Moroccan spice blend; cook until browned and fragrant, about 2 minutes. Season with salt and pepper. Remove lamb using a slotted spoon, reserving drippings in pan.

3. Toss carrots in hot drippings in skillet, and sauté for 1 minute. Transfer skillet to oven.

4. Bake, stirring carrots once, until golden and tender, 15 to 18 minutes.

5. In a large bowl, combine kale and ¼ cup Lemon-Tahini Vinaigrette, using your fingers to massage kale until tender and well coated. Toss in frisée and parsley.

6. Divide salad among 4 serving dishes. Top with lamb mixture, carrots, pomegranate arils, and pine nuts. Serve warm with remaining Lemon-Tahini Vinaigrette.

FOR LEMON-TAHINI VINAIGRETTE

1. In a glass jar with a tight-fitting lid, combine mint, oil, lemon juice, tahini, 2 tablespoons water, and shallot. Shake vigorously until well combined. Season with salt and pepper. Let stand for 20 minutes before serving to allow flavors to blend.

BEET AND ARUGULA SALAD

MAKES 4 TO 6 SERVINGS

Arugula makes a lovely base for this salad, which is packed with grapefruit, crunchy fennel, and earthy beets.

- **3 small golden beets, trimmed and scrubbed**
- **¼ (8-ounce) block feta cheese, crumbled (about ½ cup)**
- **½ cup plain whole Greek yogurt**
- **2 tablespoons whole milk**
- **2 tablespoons white balsamic vinegar**
- **2 tablespoons olive oil**
- **½ teaspoon kosher salt**
- **⅛ teaspoon toasted fennel seeds, crushed**
- **⅛ teaspoon crushed red pepper**
- **1 cup shaved fennel bulb**
- **5 cups loosely packed fresh baby arugula**
- **1 cup lightly packed torn fresh radicchio leaves**
- **1 large grapefruit, peeled, halved, sliced, and seeded**

Garnish: crushed red pepper

1. Preheat oven to 400°.
2. Wrap beets in foil, and place on a rimmed baking sheet.
3. Bake until fork-tender, 45 minutes to 1 hour. Let cool completely. Unwrap beets. Using foil, rub skin off beets. Slice beets into small wedges.
4. In the work bowl of a food processor, combine feta and yogurt, and process until smooth, stopping to scrape sides of bowl. Add milk, 1 tablespoon at a time, to thin mixture, if needed. Spoon onto serving platter.
5. In a large bowl, whisk together vinegar, oil, salt, fennel seed, and red pepper. Add beets and shaved fennel; toss until coated. Add arugula and radicchio leaves, and toss until coated. Place mixture on top of feta mixture. Place grapefruit on top. Garnish with red pepper, if desired. Serve immediately.

GREENS AND CORNBREAD SALAD

MAKES 6 SERVINGS

Inspired by Italian panzanella, this hearty salad brings a taste of the South's bounty to the table.

FOR SALAD
- 7 cups (1-inch) cubed cornbread
- 3 cups chopped stemmed fresh kale
- 3 cups chopped fresh beet greens
- 2 cups fresh arugula
- 1 cup halved assorted cherry tomatoes
- ¼ cup thinly sliced red onion
- Tangy Buttermilk Dressing (recipe follows)

FOR TANGY BUTTERMILK DRESSING
- ¾ cup whole buttermilk
- 2 tablespoons finely chopped fresh basil
- 2 tablespoons finely chopped green onion
- 2 tablespoons extra-virgin olive oil
- 2 tablespoons fresh lime juice
- 1 tablespoon finely chopped fresh parsley
- 1 tablespoon honey
- 1 tablespoon hot sauce
- ½ teaspoon kosher salt

FOR SALAD

1. Preheat oven to 450°.

2. Spread cornbread cubes onto a baking sheet. Bake until toasted, about 20 minutes, turning halfway through.

3. In a large bowl, gently toss together toasted cornbread cubes, kale, beet greens, arugula, tomatoes, and onion. Drizzle with Tangy Buttermilk Dressing; toss gently. Serve immediately.

FOR TANGY BUTTERMILK DRESSING

1. In a small bowl, whisk together all ingredients until combined. Refrigerate for up to 2 days.

CRISPY KALE SALAD WITH ROASTED SWEET POTATOES

MAKES 6 TO 8 SERVINGS

Salad will be everyone's comfort go-to when you layer in flavorful sweet potatoes and crispy cornbread croutons. You'll be craving this dish all year long.

FOR SALAD

- 4 cups chopped fresh curly kale
- 3 cups chopped fresh red kale
- 3 cups chopped fresh lacinato kale (Tuscan kale)
- 2 tablespoons olive oil, divided
- 1 tablespoon kosher salt, divided
- 3 cups peeled and ½-inch diced sweet potato
- 3 cups (¾-inch) cubed Buttermilk Cornbread (recipe follows)
- ¼ cup grated Parmigiano-Reggiano cheese
- 2 cups fresh baby kale
- ¼ cup sliced red onion
- ¼ cup toasted chopped pecans
- ½ cup mayonnaise
- ¼ cup balsamic vinegar
- 2 tablespoons pure maple syrup
- 1 tablespoon Dijon mustard

FOR BUTTERMILK CORNBREAD

- ½ cup unsalted butter, diced
- 2 cups stone-ground cornmeal
- 1 cup all-purpose flour
- 1 tablespoon baking powder
- 1 tablespoon sugar
- 1½ teaspoons kosher salt
- 2½ cups whole buttermilk
- 2 large eggs

FOR SALAD

1. Preheat oven to 375°. Line 3 rimmed baking sheets with parchment paper.

2. In a large bowl, combine curly kale, red kale, and lacinato kale. Transfer half of kale mixture to another bowl. To half of kale mixture, add 1 tablespoon oil and 1½ teaspoons salt, tossing until well combined. Transfer to a prepared baking sheet.

3. Bake until browned and crisp, 13 to 15 minutes. Let cool completely.

4. In a medium bowl, toss together sweet potato, remaining 1 tablespoon oil, and remaining 1½ teaspoons salt. Transfer to another prepared baking sheet.

5. Bake, turning occasionally, until golden brown and tender, 25 to 30 minutes. Let cool completely.

6. Reduce oven temperature to 350°. Arrange Buttermilk Cornbread cubes on remaining prepared baking sheet. Sprinkle with Parmigiano-Reggiano. Bake until golden brown and crisp, 35 to 40 minutes.

7. To remaining half of kale mixture, add roasted kale, roasted sweet potatoes, cornbread croutons, baby kale, red onion, and pecans.

8. In a small bowl, whisk together mayonnaise, vinegar, maple syrup, and mustard. Drizzle over kale mixture, and gently toss to combine.

FOR BUTTERMILK CORNBREAD

1. Preheat oven to 425°. Place a 10-inch cast-iron skillet in oven to preheat, at least 15 minutes.

2. Place butter in the cast-iron skillet and return to oven to melt. In a large bowl, whisk together cornmeal, flour, baking powder, sugar, and salt.

3. In a small bowl, whisk together buttermilk and eggs. Stir buttermilk mixture into cornmeal mixture until just combined. Slowly pour melted butter into batter, stirring until well combined. Pour batter into preheated skillet.

4. Bake until golden brown and a wooden pick inserted in center comes out clean, 25 to 30 minutes. Let cool in pan for 5 minutes. Invert cornbread onto a wire rack, and let cool completely.

BROWN RICE SALAD

MAKES 8 TO 10 SERVINGS

This salad is delicious served warm, at room temperature, or chilled, making it a great choice for meal prepping or taking to a New Year's Day potluck.

- 2 cups water
- 1 cup brown rice*
- 1 teaspoon kosher salt, divided
- 1 large Honeycrisp apple, cored and sliced ¼-inch thick
- 1 (15.5-ounce) can black-eyed peas, rinsed and drained
- 4 cups fresh baby spinach
- ½ cup dried cranberries
- ½ cup chopped toasted walnuts
- ¼ cup chopped green onion
- 3 tablespoons fresh lemon juice
- 1½ tablespoons country-style Dijon mustard
- ¾ teaspoon garlic powder
- ¾ teaspoon ground black pepper
- 6 tablespoons olive oil
- Garnish: chopped green onion, chopped walnuts

1. Line a large rimmed baking sheet with parchment paper.

2. In a medium saucepan, bring 2 cups water, rice, and ¼ teaspoon salt to a boil over medium-high heat. Cover, reduce heat to medium-low, and cook until tender, about 20 minutes. Remove from heat, and let sit, covered, for 5 minutes. Fluff with a fork; place in an even layer on prepared pan. Let cool at room temperature for 15 minutes.

3. In a large bowl, toss together cooled rice, apple, black-eyed peas, spinach, cranberries, walnuts, and green onion.

4. In a small bowl, whisk together lemon juice, mustard, garlic powder, pepper, and remaining ¾ teaspoon salt. Gradually whisk in oil until smooth. Add ½ cup dressing to salad, tossing to coat. Serve with remaining ¼ cup dressing. Garnish with green onion and walnuts, if desired.

**We used Anson Mills Charleston Gold Brown Rice.*

MAINS

chapter 3

POT ROAST WITH RED WINE COCOA GRAVY

MAKES ABOUT 6 SERVINGS

Cocoa powder, red wine, and fresh rosemary combine to create this soul-soothing, melt-in your-mouth dish.

- **2 tablespoons vegetable oil**
- **1 (3½-pound) boneless chuck roast, trimmed**
- **2¾ teaspoons kosher salt, divided**
- **1 teaspoon ground black pepper, plus more for sprinkling**
- **1 medium yellow onion, cut into 8 wedges**
- **2½ tablespoons unsweetened cocoa powder**
- **1½ cups dry red wine**
- **½ cup crushed tomatoes**
- **2 tablespoons minced garlic**
- **1 tablespoon minced fresh rosemary**
- **¼ cup all-purpose flour**

Garnish: chopped fresh rosemary

1. On an electric pressure cooker, select SAUTÉ feature. Add oil to pressure cooker pot, and heat until hot. Sprinkle beef with 2½ teaspoons salt and pepper. Add beef to pot; cook until browned, about 3 minutes per side. Remove beef from pot. Add removable trivet to pot, according to manufacturer's instructions. Return beef to pot. Add onion.

2. In a medium bowl, whisk together cocoa, wine, tomatoes, garlic, and rosemary. Pour over beef. Select CANCEL feature. Cover and lock lid. Select MANUAL feature. Pressure-cook on HIGH for 1 hour and 15 minutes. Quick release pressure. Uncover; remove beef, and place on a serving plate (see Kitchen Tip). Strain cooking liquid; return to pot.

3. In a small bowl, whisk together flour and remaining ¼ teaspoon salt. Whisk in 1 cup cooking liquid. Whisk flour mixture into remaining cooking liquid in pot. Select SAUTÉ feature. Cook for about 3 minutes, whisking constantly, until thickened and bubbly. Serve with beef. Sprinkle with additional pepper. Garnish with rosemary, if desired.

KITCHEN TIP The roast is done when a sharp knife can be easily inserted through the center. If it still isn't quite tender yet, cover and lock lid. Pressure-cook for a few more minutes.

SLOW COOKER DIRECTIONS In a large skillet, heat oil over medium-high heat. Sprinkle beef with 2½ teaspoons salt and pepper. Add beef to skillet; cook until browned, about 3 minutes per side. Place in a 6-quart slow cooker. Add onion. In a medium bowl, whisk together cocoa, wine, tomatoes, garlic, and rosemary. Pour over beef. Cover and cook on low for 9 hours. Remove beef. Strain cooking liquid into a medium saucepan. In a small bowl, whisk together 3 tablespoons flour and remaining ¼ teaspoon salt. Whisk flour mixture into remaining cooking liquid in saucepan. Cook over medium heat, whisking constantly, until thickened and bubbly. Serve with beef. Sprinkle with additional pepper. Garnish with rosemary, if desired.

SUNDAY POT ROAST WITH CREAMY CHEDDAR CHEESE GRITS

MAKES 6 SERVINGS

Your family will come running for a taste of this rich Sunday supper star.

FOR POT ROAST

- 1 (3- to 4-pound) boneless chuck roast, trimmed
- 3 teaspoons kosher salt, divided
- 1 teaspoon ground black pepper, divided
- 3 tablespoons vegetable oil
- 1 (15.5-ounce) can crushed tomatoes
- 1 (32-ounce) container beef broth
- 4 large sprigs fresh thyme
- 3 bay leaves
- 2 tablespoons finely chopped fresh rosemary
- 4 large carrots, peeled, halved lengthwise, and cut into 3-inch pieces
- 3 large stalks celery, cut into 3-inch pieces
- 3 cloves garlic, halved
- 1 large yellow onion, cut into 8 wedges
- 1 tablespoon cornstarch
- 1 tablespoon cold water

Cheese Grits (recipe follows), to serve

Garnish: chopped fresh parsley, ground black pepper

FOR CHEESE GRITS

- 6 cups water
- ½ cup heavy whipping cream
- 1 tablespoon kosher salt
- 1 teaspoon ground black pepper
- 1½ cups stone-ground grits
- 2 tablespoons unsalted butter
- 1½ cups shredded Cheddar cheese

FOR POT ROAST

1. Preheat oven to 350°.

2. Sprinkle roast with 2 teaspoons salt and ½ teaspoon pepper.

3. In a 6-quart cast-iron Dutch oven, heat oil over medium-high heat. Add roast, and cook until browned, about 3 minutes per side. Pour tomatoes and broth over roast; add thyme, bay leaves, and rosemary.

4. Bake, covered, for about 2 hours. Arrange carrot, celery, garlic, and onion around beef. Sprinkle with remaining 1 teaspoon salt and remaining ½ teaspoon pepper. Cover and bake until roast is very tender, about 1 hour more. Discard bay leaves and thyme stems. Remove roast and vegetables, and set aside.

5. In a small bowl, whisk together cornstarch and 1 tablespoon cold water; stir into cooking liquid. Cook over medium heat until thickened and bubbly. Remove from heat; add roast and vegetables back to gravy, tossing to coat. Serve over Cheese Grits. Garnish with parsley and pepper, if desired.

FOR CHEESE GRITS

1. In a medium saucepan, bring 6 cups water, cream, salt, and pepper to a boil over medium-high heat. Slowly whisk in grits.

2. Reduce heat to medium-low. Cover, and cook, whisking frequently, until tender, about 20 minutes. Whisk in butter and cheese until melted. Serve warm.

BROWN BUTTER STEAKS AND SORGHUM RISOTTO

MAKES 2 TO 4 SERVINGS

When cooked slowly with broth, sorghum grains create a creamy risotto. It's a dish so delectable we'll be making it year-round.

- 1½ cups whole sorghum grain*
- 6 cups less-sodium chicken broth
- 4 cups water
- 5 tablespoons unsalted butter, divided
- 1 (8-ounce) container fresh baby portobello mushrooms, quartered
- 1 tablespoon chopped fresh thyme
- ½ cup dry white wine
- 1 cup grated Parmesan cheese
- 2½ teaspoons kosher salt, divided
- 1 teaspoon ground black pepper, divided
- 2 (1¼-pound) bone-in rib-eye steaks
- 2 tablespoons canola oil
- 4 sprigs fresh thyme
- 3 cloves garlic, smashed

Garnish: chopped fresh thyme, freshly ground black pepper

1. In a large bowl, place sorghum and enough water to cover by 2 inches. Cover and refrigerate overnight. Drain well.

2. In a large saucepan, bring broth and 4 cups water to a simmer over medium heat. Reduce heat to medium-low; cover and keep warm.

3. In a large Dutch oven, heat 1 tablespoon butter over medium-high heat. Add mushrooms and thyme. Cook, stirring occasionally, until golden brown, about 8 minutes. Using a slotted spoon, remove from pan and set aside.

4. Add sorghum to pan, and cook, stirring constantly, about 1 minute. Stir in 1 cup warm broth mixture; cover and cook, stirring frequently, until liquid is almost absorbed, about 5 minutes. Continue adding warm broth mixture, 1 cup at a time, covering, and cooking until liquid is almost absorbed, about 1 hour total. Stir in wine. Cover and cook, stirring occasionally, until liquid is almost absorbed, about 4 minutes. Remove from heat. Add reserved mushroom mixture, cheese, ½ teaspoon salt, and ½ teaspoon pepper, stirring until smooth. Keep warm.

5. Season both sides of steaks with remaining 2 teaspoons salt and remaining ½ teaspoon pepper; let sit at room temperature for 15 to 20 minutes.

6. In a large cast-iron skillet, heat remaining 4 tablespoons butter and oil over high heat until butter is light brown, about 3 minutes. Add seasoned steaks; cook until browned, about 5 minutes. Turn steaks, and add thyme sprigs and garlic to pan. While cooking, frequently spoon butter mixture over steaks until cooked to desired doneness, about 5 to 10 minutes more. Remove from heat. Let stand for 10 minutes before slicing. Serve steaks over sorghum risotto. Garnish with thyme and pepper, if desired.

**We used Bob's Red Mill Whole Grain Sorghum.*

JUNIPER GIN STEAK

MAKES 4 SERVINGS

Make your next steak supper even more special with this creative take.

- **5 teaspoons cracked black pepper, divided**
- **2 teaspoons kosher salt**
- **8 juniper berries, coarsely crushed and divided**
- **4 tablespoons olive oil, divided**
- **1 (1½-pound) flank steak**
- **4 tablespoons cold unsalted butter, divided**
- **¼ cup diced shallot**
- **¼ cup thinly sliced red onion**
- **¼ cup gin**
- **1 cup chicken broth**
- **¼ cup heavy whipping cream**

1. In a small bowl, combine 4½ teaspoons pepper, salt, and 1 teaspoon crushed juniper berries.

2. Rub 1 tablespoon olive oil on steak to evenly coat. Rub spice mixture over steak. Let stand for 15 minutes.

3. In a 12-inch cast-iron skillet, heat remaining 3 tablespoons oil over medium-high heat. Add steak; cook until crust forms on both sides and steak is cooked to desired doneness, 8 to 10 minutes, turning often to avoid burning and to keep crisp. Remove from pan and let rest for 5 to 10 minutes.

4. In same pan, melt 2 tablespoons butter over medium heat. Add shallot and onion; cook until softened. Add remaining ½ teaspoon crushed juniper berries, remaining ½ teaspoon pepper, and gin. Stir to combine, scraping bottom of pan to release steak drippings. Add chicken broth and cook until liquid is reduced by half. Add cream and simmer until thickened. Whisk in remaining 2 tablespoons butter, stirring until butter is melted.

5. Thinly slice steak against the grain and drizzle gin sauce over steak. Serve immediately.

BEEF SHORT RIBS WITH CHEESE GRITS

MAKES 4 TO 6 SERVINGS

Braised in wine and herbs, these slow-cooked short ribs pair perfectly with grits cooked in beef broth for even more flavor.

FOR SHORT RIBS

- 1 (750-ml) bottle Burgundy wine
- 5 tablespoons all-purpose flour, divided
- 5 pounds bone-in beef short ribs
- 2 teaspoons kosher salt, plus more to taste
- 1 teaspoon ground black pepper, plus more to taste
- 2 tablespoons olive oil
- 1 (6-ounce) can tomato paste
- 2 medium onions, thinly sliced
- 1 head garlic, halved crosswise
- 10 sprigs fresh parsley
- 8 sprigs fresh thyme
- 4 sprigs fresh oregano
- 2 sprigs fresh rosemary
- 2 bay leaves
- 2 tablespoons unsalted butter
- 1 cup less-sodium beef broth
- Cheese Grits (recipe follows), to serve
- Garnish: fresh oregano, ground black pepper

FOR CHEESE GRITS

- 4½ cups less-sodium beef broth
- 2 teaspoons kosher salt
- 1½ cups stone-ground yellow grits
- 2 cups shredded sharp Cheddar cheese
- 1 cup whole milk
- 3 tablespoons unsalted butter

FOR SHORT RIBS

1. In a medium saucepan, cook wine over medium-high heat until reduced to 2 cups, about 20 minutes.
2. Preheat oven to 350°.
3. Place 3 tablespoons flour in a shallow dish. Sprinkle short ribs with salt and pepper, and dredge in flour.
4. In a large enameled cast-iron Dutch oven, heat oil over medium-high heat. Working in batches, add short ribs to pot; cook until browned on all sides, 4 to 6 minutes. Transfer ribs to a plate. Remove pot from heat and pour off drippings.
5. In same pot, add reduced wine, scraping browned bits from bottom of pot with a wooden spoon. Whisk in tomato paste until smooth. Add onion, and top with ribs. Add garlic, parsley, thyme, oregano, rosemary, and bay leaves.
6. Cover pot and bake until short ribs are tender, 2 hours to 2 hours and 30 minutes. Transfer short ribs to a platter.
7. Strain cooking liquid from pot through a fine-mesh sieve into a measuring cup, discarding solids. Skim off fat from surface of liquid; reserve 1 cup liquid. Wipe pot clean.
8. In same pot, melt butter over medium heat. Whisk in remaining 2 tablespoons flour; cook for 1 minute. Whisk in broth and reserved 1 cup cooking liquid until thickened. Remove from heat, and season with salt and pepper. Serve short ribs with Cheese Grits, and top with sauce. Garnish with oregano and pepper, if desired.

FOR CHEESE GRITS

1. In a Dutch oven, bring broth and salt to a boil over medium-high heat; slowly stir in grits. Reduce heat to medium-low; cover and cook, stirring occasionally, until thickened, about 30 minutes.
2. Uncover and stir in cheese, milk, and butter. Serve immediately.

BRAISED SHORT RIB BOLOGNESE

MAKES 6 SERVINGS

The only way to make braised short ribs better is to pair them with pasta, so we twirled them up in tagliatelle and topped it all with shaved pecorino.

- 1½ cups dry red wine
- 3 tablespoons olive oil, divided
- 1½ teaspoons kosher salt
- 1 teaspoon ground black pepper, divided
- 2½ pounds flanken-cut beef short ribs, boned and chopped
- 1 medium sweet onion, finely chopped
- 2 cloves garlic, minced
- 1 (28-ounce) can peeled whole tomatoes, undrained
- 1 cup less-sodium beef broth
- 1 (13.2-ounce) package tagliatelle pasta
- Garnish: shaved pecorino cheese, crushed red pepper

1. In a large bowl, stir together wine, 2 tablespoons oil, salt, and ½ teaspoon pepper; stir in short ribs. Cover and refrigerate for at least 8 hours or overnight.

2. Remove beef from marinade, reserving excess liquid. In a large Dutch oven, heat remaining 1 tablespoon oil over medium-high heat. Add beef, onion, garlic, and remaining ½ teaspoon pepper; cook for 5 minutes. Add reserved marinade and tomatoes; bring to a boil. Reduce heat to medium; cover and cook until tender, about 25 minutes.

3. Add broth; return to a boil. Add pasta; cover and cook for 8 to 10 minutes. Garnish with pecorino and red pepper, if desired.

GRANDMA'S LASAGNA

MAKES 10 TO 12 SERVINGS

Stashing away a tray (or three) of this flavor-packed lasagna makes weeknight meals effortless.

- **4 slices thick-cut bacon, chopped**
- **1½ pounds ground beef**
- **1 cup chopped red onion**
- **5 cloves garlic, minced**
- **4 cups packed chopped fresh turnip greens (about ½ pound)**
- **½ cup less-sodium chicken broth**
- **2 (15-ounce) cans tomato sauce**
- **1 (14.5-ounce) can diced tomatoes, undrained**
- **3 tablespoons firmly packed light brown sugar**
- **2¾ teaspoons Cajun seasoning***
- **½ cup finely chopped fresh parsley**
- **12 lasagna noodles, cooked according to package directions**
- **4 cups shredded fontina cheese**
- **Garnish: chopped fresh parsley**

1. Preheat oven to 350°. Spray a 13x9-inch baking dish with cooking spray.

2. In a large Dutch oven, cook bacon over medium heat until crisp. Using a slotted spoon, remove bacon and let drain on paper towels, reserving 2 tablespoons drippings in pot.

3. Add beef to pot; cook, stirring frequently, until browned and crumbly, 5 to 7 minutes. Transfer beef to a medium bowl, reserving drippings in pot.

4. Add onion and garlic to pot; cook, stirring frequently, until softened, 3 to 4 minutes. Add half of greens; cook for 1 minute, stirring frequently. Stir in broth and remaining greens; bring to a boil. Partially cover and cook for 5 minutes, stirring occasionally. Uncover and cook until greens are tender and liquid is mostly evaporated, about 3 minutes. Add tomato sauce, tomatoes, brown sugar, and Cajun seasoning, stirring to combine; cook until heated through, about 5 minutes. Stir in bacon, beef, and parsley.

5. Spread one-fourth of beef mixture in prepared pan. Layer with 4 noodles, overlapping as needed; cover with another fourth of beef mixture, and top with one-third of cheese. Repeat layers twice, starting with noodles.

6. Bake until filling is bubbly, about 40 minutes. Uncover and bake until lightly browned on top, 5 to 10 minutes more. Let stand for 20 minutes before serving. Garnish with parsley, if desired.

**We used Slap Ya Mama Original Blend Cajun Seasoning.*

STOVETOP LASAGNA

MAKES 6 TO 8 SERVINGS

Cheesy lasagna gets a one-dish makeover for an easy version of the beloved meal.

- 2 tablespoons olive oil
- 1 pound ground mild Italian sausage
- 2 cups diced white onion
- 1 tablespoon tomato paste
- 1 tablespoon minced garlic
- 1 teaspoon kosher salt, divided
- 1 teaspoon Italian seasoning, divided
- ¾ teaspoon ground black pepper, divided
- ⅛ teaspoon crushed red pepper
- 1 (28-ounce) can crushed tomatoes
- 1 (14-ounce) can diced tomatoes
- 2 tablespoons chopped fresh basil
- 1 (15-ounce) container whole milk ricotta cheese
- ¾ cup grated Parmesan cheese, divided
- 1 large egg, lightly beaten
- 6 sheets no-bake lasagna noodles, broken into pieces
- 2 cups shredded Italian cheese blend, divided

Garnish: fresh basil leaves

1. Preheat oven to 375°

2. In a 10-inch enameled cast-iron skillet, heat oil over medium heat. Cook and crumble sausage until browned. Add onion, and cook, stirring occasionally, until tender, 5 to 7 minutes. Stir in tomato paste, garlic, ½ teaspoon salt, ½ teaspoon Italian seasoning, ½ teaspoon black pepper, and red pepper; stirring until blended, about 1 minute. Stir in all tomatoes and basil, and bring to a boil. Reduce heat to low, and simmer, stirring frequently, until sauce is slightly reduced, about 15 minutes. Transfer sauce to large bowl.

3. In a medium bowl, whisk together ricotta, ½ cup Parmesan, egg, remaining ½ teaspoon salt, remaining ½ teaspoon Italian seasoning, and remaining ¼ teaspoon black pepper.

4. In same skillet, spoon one-third meat sauce in bottom. Top with one-third noodle pieces in a single layer, overlapping as needed. Spread one-third of ricotta mixture onto noodles. Spread one-third of meat sauce onto ricotta mixture; sprinkle with ½ cup Italian cheese blend. Starting with noodles, repeat layers twice. Sprinkle with remaining ¼ cup Parmesan cheese and remaining ½ cup Italian cheese blend.

5. Bake until cheese is melted and top is lightly browned, 35 to 40 minutes. Let stand for 10 minutes before serving. Garnish with basil, if desired.

PECAN-CRUSTED CATFISH

MAKES 6 SERVINGS

Fried catfish is a favorite cozy meal, and this version adds a hint of salty pecan to the classic crunchy crust.

FOR CATFISH

Vegetable oil, for frying
- 1 cup whole buttermilk
- 2 teaspoons hot sauce, plus more to serve
- 3 cups plain yellow or white cornmeal
- 1 cup all-purpose flour
- 1 cup very finely chopped pecans
- 1½ tablespoons kosher salt
- 1½ teaspoons garlic powder
- ½ cup cornstarch
- 6 (6-ounce) catfish fillets

Lemon wedges, to serve
Pecan Herb Dipping Sauce (recipe follows), to serve
Garnish: fresh parsley

FOR PECAN HERB DIPPING SAUCE

- ½ cup toasted pecans
- 3 tablespoons chopped fresh parsley
- 1 clove garlic, chopped
- ⅓ cup olive oil
- 1 teaspoon lemon zest
- 1 tablespoon fresh lemon juice
- 2 teaspoons chopped fresh dill
- 1 teaspoon kosher salt
- ¼ teaspoon crushed red pepper

FOR CATFISH

1. In a large cast-iron skillet, pour oil to a depth of 1½ inches, and heat over medium heat until a deep-fry thermometer registers 350°. Place a wire rack on a rimmed baking sheet.

2. In a medium bowl, combine buttermilk and hot sauce. In a large shallow dish, whisk together cornmeal, flour, pecans, salt, and garlic powder. In another shallow bowl, place cornstarch. Working in batches, dredge catfish in cornstarch; dip in buttermilk mixture, letting excess drip off, and dredge in cornmeal mixture, pressing to adhere.

3. Working in batches, fry catfish, turning occasionally, until golden brown, about 4 minutes. Remove from oil, and let drain on prepared rack. Serve with hot sauce, lemon wedges, and Pecan Herb Dipping Sauce. Garnish with parsley, if desired.

FOR PECAN HERB DIPPING SAUCE

1. In the work bowl of a food processor, combine pecans, parsley, and garlic; pulse until finely chopped. Transfer to a medium bowl.

2. Stir in oil, lemon zest and juice, dill, salt, and red pepper.

LAMB OSSO BUCO WITH GREMOLATA

MAKES 4 SERVINGS

This recipe is the gift that keeps on giving! It makes a generous amount of sauce you can save for later. (Spoiler alert: it goes great with pasta.)

FOR LAMB

- 4 tablespoons vegetable oil, divided
- 1½ cups coarsely chopped carrot
- ⅔ cup chopped celery
- ½ cup chopped yellow onion
- 4 teaspoons minced garlic
- 4 lamb shanks (about 3 pounds)
- 1½ teaspoons kosher salt, divided
- ½ teaspoon ground black pepper
- 1 cup dry white wine
- 1 (15-ounce) can crushed tomatoes
- Gremolata (recipe follows), for sprinkling

FOR GREMOLATA

- ⅓ cup chopped fresh parsley
- 2 teaspoons minced garlic
- 1 teaspoon lemon zest

FOR LAMB

1. On an electric pressure cooker, select SAUTÉ feature. Add 2 tablespoons oil to cooking pot, and heat until hot. Add carrot, celery, and onion; sauté until lightly browned, about 4 minutes. Add garlic; sauté for 1 minute. Remove carrot mixture.

2. Add remaining 2 tablespoons oil to pot. Sprinkle lamb with 1¼ teaspoons salt and pepper. Add half of lamb to pot; cook, turning occasionally, until browned, about 6 minutes. Remove lamb from pot. Repeat with remaining lamb.

3. Add wine to pot, scraping browned bits from bottom of pot with a wooden spoon. Stir in tomatoes and carrot mixture. Add lamb, and spoon some sauce over lamb. Select CANCEL feature. Cover and lock lid. Select MANUAL feature. Pressure-cook on HIGH for 35 minutes. Quick release pressure. Uncover; remove lamb, and place on a serving plate.

4. Select SAUTÉ feature. Cook tomato mixture for 5 minutes. Stir in remaining ¼ teaspoon salt. Serve over lamb. Sprinkle with Gremolata.

FOR GREMOLATA

1. In a small bowl, toss together all ingredients. Use immediately.

SLOW COOKER DIRECTIONS In a large skillet, heat 2 tablespoons oil over medium-high heat. Add carrot, celery, and onion; sauté until lightly browned, about 4 minutes. Add garlic; sauté for 1 minute. Remove from skillet. Heat remaining 2 tablespoons oil over medium heat. Sprinkle lamb with 1¼ teaspoons salt and pepper. Add lamb to skillet; cook, turning occasionally, until browned, about 6 minutes. Remove lamb. Add wine, scraping browned bits from bottom of pan with a wooden spoon. Stir in tomatoes and carrot mixture. Place lamb in a 6-quart slow cooker. Add tomato mixture. Cover and cook on low for 6 hours. Remove lamb. Cover and cook tomato mixture on high for 10 minutes. Stir in remaining ¼ teaspoon salt. Serve over lamb. Sprinkle with Gremolata.

PIMIENTO CHEESE GRITS WITH PORK CHOPS AND MUSHROOMS

MAKES 2 SERVINGS

With creamy cheese grits and hearty pork chops, these grits bowls are comfort food at its finest. To have everything ready at once, start cooking the pork chops 20 minutes into the grits cooking time.

- 3¼ cups water, divided
- 1¾ teaspoons kosher salt, divided
- ½ teaspoon ground black pepper, divided
- ¾ cup stone-ground grits
- 3 tablespoons vegetable oil, divided
- 2 (¾-inch-thick) pork rib chops
- 1 (8-ounce) package fresh cremini mushrooms, sliced
- ½ cup chopped onion
- 2 teaspoons chopped fresh thyme
- ¾ cup shredded sharp Cheddar cheese
- 2 tablespoons heavy whipping cream
- ½ teaspoon hot sauce
- 1 (4-ounce) jar diced pimientos, drained
- Garnish: chopped fresh thyme, ground black pepper

1. In a large saucepan, bring 3 cups water, 1 teaspoon salt, and ¼ teaspoon pepper to a boil over medium-high heat. Gradually stir in grits; reduce heat to medium-low. Partially cover and cook, stirring occasionally, until thickened and tender, about 40 minutes.

2. Meanwhile, in a medium skillet, heat 2 tablespoons oil over medium-high heat. Sprinkle pork chops with ½ teaspoon salt and remaining ¼ teaspoon pepper. Add chops to skillet; cook until a meat thermometer inserted in thickest portion registers 145°, 3 to 4 minutes per side. Remove from skillet. Loosely cover pork chops.

3. Heat remaining 1 tablespoon oil over medium-high heat. Add mushrooms and onion; sprinkle with remaining ¼ teaspoon salt. Cook, stirring frequently, until mushrooms release their liquid and are tender, about 5 minutes. Add thyme and remaining ¼ cup water, scraping browned bits from bottom of pan with a wooden spoon.

4. Remove grits from heat; stir in cheese, cream, and hot sauce until smooth. Stir in pimientos. Serve grits with pork chops and mushroom mixture. Garnish with thyme and pepper, if desired.

PORK CHOPS AND MASHED POTATOES

MAKES 4 SERVINGS

If you're craving a meal that feels like home, look no further than this cozy dinner.

- 1 tablespoon olive oil
- 4 (9- to 10-ounce) thick-cut bone-in pork chops
- 1 tablespoon plus ½ teaspoon kosher salt, divided
- 2 tablespoons unsalted butter
- 4 cups thinly sliced yellow onion
- 1 cup beef broth, divided
- 2 (8-ounce) containers sliced fresh portobello mushrooms
- 1 tablespoon minced garlic
- 2 sprigs fresh thyme
- 1 teaspoon paprika
- 1½ cups heavy whipping cream
- ¼ cup dry sherry
- Mashed potatoes, to serve
- Garnish: fresh thyme, fresh parsley

1. In a large enameled cast-iron braiser, heat oil over medium-high heat. Pat pork chops dry with paper towels, and sprinkle with 1 tablespoon salt. Add to pan, and cook until browned on both sides, 7 to 10 minutes. Remove from pan.
2. In same pan, melt butter over medium heat. Add onion, and cook, stirring frequently, until onion begins to stick to pan. Add ¼ cup beef broth, scraping bottom of pan to remove any stuck bits. Repeat until onion is deep golden brown and very tender, 15 to 20 minutes.
3. Add mushrooms, garlic, and remaining ¾ cup beef broth. Cook, stirring occasionally, until tender and most of liquid has reduced, 5 to 7 minutes. Stir in thyme, paprika, cream, and sherry. Cook, stirring occasionally, until thickened and coats the back of a spoon, 7 to 10 minutes. Return pork chops to pan, and cook, stirring occasionally, until heated through and an instant-read thermometer registers 155°, 10 to 12 minutes. Discard thyme sprigs.
4. Serve over mashed potatoes. Garnish with thyme and parsley, if desired.

COCONUT MILK SMOTHERED PORK TENDERLOIN MEDALLIONS

MAKES 4 SERVINGS

Chinese five-spice powder combines with a creamy coconut milk sauce to create this tasty and rich pork main dish. Serve it over hot cooked rice, if desired.

- 1 large egg, lightly beaten
- ½ cup all-purpose flour
- 1 tablespoon Chinese five-spice powder
- 1½ teaspoons kosher salt, divided
- 1 (1-pound) pork tenderloin, cut into 1-inch medallions
- 3 tablespoons coconut oil
- 2 (3.5-ounce) containers fresh shiitake mushrooms, stemmed and halved
- 8 green onions, cut into 2-inch pieces
- ¾ cup coconut milk
- ¼ cup heavy whipping cream

Garnish: Thai basil leaves

1. Place egg in a small bowl. In a shallow dish, combine flour, five-spice powder, and 1 teaspoon salt. Dip pork medallions in egg, letting excess drip off. Dredge in flour mixture, shaking off excess.

2. In a large skillet, heat oil over medium-high heat. Add pork; cook until browned, about 3 minutes per side. Remove from pan, and set aside.

3. Add mushrooms and green onion to pan; cook until mushrooms begin to brown, about 2 minutes. Return pork to pan. Stir in coconut milk, cream, and remaining ½ teaspoon salt. Reduce heat to medium-low; cook until sauce begins to thicken, about 5 minutes. Garnish with basil, if desired.

BROCCOLI, HAM AND CHEDDAR COBBLER

MAKES 6 TO 8 SERVINGS

Protein, veggies, and carbs come together to create this indulgent all-in-one recipe.

- 1 tablespoon olive oil
- 4 cups diced ham
- ¼ cup unsalted butter
- ¼ cup all-purpose flour
- 2 cups whole milk
- 2½ teaspoons kosher salt, divided
- 1 cup heavy whipping cream
- 4 cups chopped fresh broccoli
- 3 cups shredded sharp Cheddar cheese, divided
- 2 cups self-rising flour
- 1 teaspoon sugar
- ½ teaspoon baking soda
- 6 tablespoons cold unsalted butter, grated
- 1⅓ cups whole buttermilk
- 3 tablespoons minced fresh chives
- Garnish: minced fresh chives

1. Preheat oven to 425°.

2. In a 12-inch skillet, heat oil over medium heat. Add ham, and cook, stirring occasionally, until lightly browned, 7 to 10 minutes. Remove from skillet.

3. In same skillet, melt ¼ cup butter over medium heat. Whisk in all-purpose flour. Cook, whisking constantly, until aromatic and lightly toasted, about 1 minute. While whisking constantly, gradually add milk until fully combined and smooth. Whisk in 2 teaspoons salt and cream. Cook, stirring frequently, until thickened, 3 to 5 minutes. Remove from heat, and stir in ham, broccoli, and 2 cups Cheddar cheese until just combined. Pour into a 13x9-inch baking dish.

4. In a medium bowl, whisk together self-rising flour, sugar, baking soda, and remaining ½ teaspoon salt. Whisk in grated butter and remaining 1 cup Cheddar cheese until well coated with flour. Stir in buttermilk and chives until just combined. Using a 2-tablespoon spring-loaded scoop, scoop batter on top of ham mixture. Gently spread together without touching edges of dish.

5. Bake until golden brown and bubbly, 20 to 25 minutes. Garnish with chives, if desired.

CAMPANELLE WITH VODKA SAUCE

MAKES 6 TO 8 SERVINGS

Pasta night just got a whole lot better thanks to this scratch-made sauce.

- 2 tablespoons olive oil
- 1 pound chopped bacon
- 1 cup finely chopped shallot
- 2 tablespoons kosher salt
- 1 tablespoon finely chopped garlic (about 4 cloves)
- 1 teaspoon sugar
- 1 teaspoon ground black pepper
- 1 teaspoon finely chopped fresh oregano
- ¼ teaspoon crushed red pepper
- 1 cup vodka
- 1 (28-ounce) can peeled San Marzano tomatoes
- 1 (28-ounce) can crushed San Marzano tomatoes
- 1 cup heavy whipping cream
- ¼ cup grated Parmesan cheese
- 1 (12-ounce) package campanelle pasta, cooked according to package instructions

Garnish: grated Parmesan cheese, torn fresh basil, chopped fresh oregano

1. In a small Dutch oven, heat oil over medium heat. Add bacon and cook until crispy, 5 to 10 minutes. Using a slotted spoon, remove bacon and let drain on paper towels, reserving ¼ cup bacon drippings in pot. Reserve ½ cup bacon.

2. Return ½ cup bacon to drippings in pan and heat over medium heat. Add shallot, salt, garlic, sugar, black pepper, oregano, and red pepper; cook until shallot is softened. Add vodka and cook until reduced by half. Add tomatoes, using a wooden spoon or spatula to break up any large pieces. Reduce heat to medium-low and simmer until sauce has thickened, 15 to 20 minutes. Add cream and Parmesan; cook until creamy and heated through, 5 to 10 minutes.

3. Serve over pasta; sprinkle with reserved ½ cup bacon. Garnish with Parmesan, basil, and oregano, if desired.

Tito's.

FIG, BACON, AND SAGE RAVIOLI

MAKES 4 SERVINGS

This flavor-filled recipe is the perfect main dish for a cozy supper.

- 4 slices thick-cut bacon, chopped (about 6 ounces)
- 1 tablespoon packed whole sage leaves
- 8 fresh figs, quartered
- ½ cup finely chopped red onion
- 4 cloves garlic, minced
- ¼ cup apple cider vinegar
- ¾ cup heavy whipping cream
- ¾ teaspoon kosher salt
- ½ teaspoon lemon zest
- ½ teaspoon ground black pepper
- ⅛ teaspoon ground nutmeg
- 2 (8-ounce) packages cheese ravioli, cooked according to package directions
- ¼ cup chopped toasted pecans

Garnish: ground black pepper

1. In a 12-inch skillet, cook bacon over medium heat until crisp. Using a slotted spoon, remove bacon and let drain on paper towels, reserving drippings in skillet.

2. Add sage to skillet; cook, stirring occasionally, until sage is crisp but still green, 30 seconds to 1 minute. Using a slotted spoon, remove sage and let drain on paper towels.

3. Add figs to skillet; cook, stirring occasionally, until figs are softened and just slightly caramelized, 2 to 3 minutes. Using a slotted spoon, transfer figs to a medium bowl.

4. Add onion and garlic to skillet; cook, stirring occasionally, until softened, 3 to 4 minutes. Pour in vinegar; cook until evaporated, 2 to 3 minutes. Stir in cream, salt, zest, pepper, and nutmeg; cook, stirring occasionally, until thickened, 1 to 2 minutes.

5. Add ravioli to cream mixture, stirring to coat. Divide pasta among 4 serving plates. Top evenly with figs, bacon, and sage; sprinkle with pecans. Garnish with pepper, if desired.

SALT-CRUSTED HOT CHICKEN

MAKES 6 TO 8 SERVINGS

Roasting this chicken under a crust of rock salt and egg whites keeps the moisture and seasonings in the meat, resulting in a juicy and flavorful bird.

- **4 cups water**
- **2½ cups whole buttermilk**
- **½ cup plus 2 teaspoons firmly packed light brown sugar, divided**
- **10 sprigs fresh thyme**
- **4 bay leaves**
- **1 (3-pound) whole chicken**
- **¼ cup canola oil**
- **2 tablespoons ground red pepper**
- **1 teaspoon dry mustard**
- **½ teaspoon smoked paprika**
- **½ teaspoon garlic powder**
- **½ teaspoon ground black pepper**
- **3 pounds rock salt**
- **4 large egg whites**

1. In a large bowl, stir together 4 cups water, buttermilk, ½ cup brown sugar, thyme, and bay leaves until sugar is dissolved. Place chicken in buttermilk mixture, breast side down. Cover and refrigerate for at least 4 hours or up to 12 hours.
2. Preheat oven to 350°.
3. Remove chicken, thyme, and bay leaves from bowl; discard brine. Place thyme and bay leaves in cavity of chicken. Pat chicken dry.
4. In a small saucepan, heat oil over medium-high heat. Add red pepper, mustard, paprika, garlic powder, black pepper, and remaining 2 teaspoons brown sugar, stirring to combine; cook until fragrant, about 1 minute. Brush pepper oil all over chicken. Place chicken in a 12-inch cast-iron chicken fryer or a medium Dutch oven.
5. In a large bowl, stir together rock salt and egg whites. Pack salt mixture onto chicken, ensuring there are no gaps in salt mixture.
6. Bake until salt is firm to the touch, about 1 hour and 15 minutes. Let stand for 15 minutes. Crack salt layer, remove chicken, and serve.

ROASTED CHICKEN THIGHS WITH HERBS AND RED ONION

MAKES 6 SERVINGS

Crispy chicken skin and fragrant herbs pack this one-skillet supper with incredible flavor. Break this recipe out for an impressive and easy dinner-party entrée.

- 6 bone-in skin-on chicken thighs
- 1½ teaspoons kosher salt
- 1 teaspoon ground black pepper
- ¼ cup plus 3 tablespoons olive oil, divided
- 1 medium red onion, cut into ¼-inch-thick slices (about 2 cups)
- 4 Fuyu persimmons, cut into wedges
- 3 sprigs fresh rosemary
- 3 sprigs fresh thyme
- ¼ cup sorghum syrup
- 1 teaspoon chopped fresh rosemary
- 1 teaspoon chopped fresh thyme

Garnish: fresh thyme sprigs, fresh rosemary sprigs

1. Preheat oven to 375°.
2. Let chicken stand at room temperature for 20 minutes. Sprinkle with salt and pepper.
3. In a 12-inch cast-iron skillet, heat 3 tablespoons oil over medium-high heat. Add chicken, skin side down; cook until browned, 6 to 8 minutes. Turn chicken over; add onion, persimmons, and herb sprigs to pan. Cook until chicken is browned, about 3 minutes. Remove from heat.
4. In a small bowl, whisk together syrup, chopped herbs, and remaining ¼ cup oil. Brush half of glaze onto chicken.
5. Bake until an instant-read thermometer inserted in thickest portion registers 165°, 30 to 40 minutes, brushing with remaining glaze halfway through baking. Garnish with thyme and rosemary, if desired.

BALSAMIC BRAISED CHICKEN THIGHS WITH PARMESAN GRITS

MAKES 4 SERVINGS

Nutty Parmesan cheese in the grits is a tasty complement to the herby, vinegar-infused chicken.

FOR CHICKEN

- 1 tablespoon vegetable oil
- 1½ teaspoons kosher salt
- 1 teaspoon ground black pepper
- 6 large bone-in skin-on chicken thighs (about 3 pounds), trimmed
- 6 large shallots (about ½ pound), peeled and halved
- 2 teaspoons minced fresh rosemary
- ½ cup balsamic vinegar
- ½ cup less-sodium chicken broth
- Parmesan Grits (recipe follows), to serve
- Garnish: fresh rosemary sprigs, ground black pepper

FOR PARMESAN GRITS

- 4 cups less-sodium chicken broth
- 1 teaspoon kosher salt
- ½ teaspoon ground black pepper
- 1 cup stone-ground white grits
- ¾ cup freshly grated Parmesan cheese (3 ounces)
- ⅓ cup heavy whipping cream
- 2 tablespoons unsalted butter

FOR CHICKEN

1. Preheat oven to 350°.

2. In a 12-inch cast-iron braiser, heat oil over medium-high heat. Sprinkle salt and pepper all over chicken. Add chicken to pan, and cook until browned, about 3 minutes per side. Remove from pan, reserving 1 tablespoon drippings in pan.

3. Add shallots to drippings in pan; cook until browned, about 3 minutes. Return chicken, skin side up, to pan. Sprinkle with rosemary. Drizzle vinegar and broth around chicken. Cover pan.

4. Bake until an instant-read thermometer inserted in the thickest portion of thighs registers 165°, about 30 minutes. Serve chicken, shallots, and pan juices with Parmesan Grits. Garnish with rosemary and pepper, if desired.

FOR PARMESAN GRITS

1. In a small enameled cast-iron Dutch oven, bring broth, salt, and pepper to a boil over medium-high heat. Slowly whisk in grits until combined. Reduce heat, and partially cover; simmer, stirring occasionally, until tender, about 40 minutes. Remove from heat.

2. Stir in cheese, cream, and butter until melted. Let stand until thickened, 5 to 10 minutes, before serving.

ORANGE-GLAZED CHICKEN

MAKES 4 TO 6 SERVINGS

Who needs takeout when you can make this irresistible recipe in less than an hour?

FOR CHICKEN

- 1 (4- to 5-pound) whole chicken, cut into 10 pieces
- 2 tablespoons olive oil
- 1 tablespoon kosher salt
- 1 teaspoon ground black pepper
- ¼ cup sliced green onion
- ¼ cup firmly packed light brown sugar
- 1 tablespoon minced garlic
- 1 tablespoon minced fresh ginger
- 1 tablespoon chili powder
- ¼ teaspoon crushed red pepper
- 1 cup orange marmalade
- ¼ cup apple cider vinegar
- ¼ cup chili sauce
- ¼ cup less-sodium soy sauce
- Broiled Green Beans (recipe follows), to serve
- Hot cooked white rice, to serve
- Garnish: sliced green onion

FOR BROILED GREEN BEANS

- 1½ pounds green beans, trimmed
- 1 tablespoon olive oil
- 1 teaspoon kosher salt

FOR CHICKEN

1. Preheat oven to 400°. Line a rimmed baking sheet with foil.

2. Arrange chicken in an even layer on prepared baking sheet. Drizzle with oil, and rub to evenly coat. Sprinkle with salt and black pepper.

3. Bake for 10 minutes.

4. In a large bowl, combine green onion, brown sugar, garlic, ginger, chili powder, crushed red pepper, orange marmalade, vinegar, chili sauce, and soy sauce. Reserve ¼ cup orange marmalade mixture to serve. Brush chicken with half remaining orange marmalade mixture.

5. Bake 15 minutes more. Brush with remaining orange marmalade mixture, and bake until golden brown, caramelized, and an instant-read thermometer inserted into chicken breast pieces registers 165° and inserted into thighs registers 170°, 10 to 15 minutes more.

6. Increase oven temperature to broil. Broil chicken until browned and bubbly, 5 to 7 minutes. Serve with Broiled Green Beans, hot cooked rice, and reserved ¼ cup orange marmalade mixture. Garnish with green onion, if desired.

FOR BROILED GREEN BEANS

1. Preheat oven to broil. Line a rimmed baking sheet with foil.

2. Drizzle green beans with oil, and sprinkle with salt. Transfer to prepared baking sheet, and broil until just tender and lightly browned, 5 to 7 minutes.

CHICKEN FLORENTINE

MAKES 6 SERVINGS

You won't miss a bite thanks to the orecchiette, which translates to "little ear" in Italian–it expertly cradles the earthy medley of mushrooms, hearty rainbow chard, and juicy chicken thighs.

- 2 tablespoons unsalted butter
- 1 pound boneless skinless chicken thighs, cut into ½-inch cubes
- 1 (4-ounce) package gourmet-blend mushrooms
- 1 bunch rainbow chard, stems and leaves separated and chopped
- 1 tablespoon all-purpose flour
- 1 (32-ounce) container less-sodium chicken broth
- ½ cup half-and-half
- 1¼ teaspoons kosher salt
- ½ teaspoon ground black pepper
- 1 (12-ounce) package orecchiette pasta

Garnish: ground black pepper

1. In a 12-inch saucepan, heat butter over medium-high heat. Add chicken; cook for 10 minutes. Add mushrooms and chard stems; cook for 5 minutes. Stir in flour; cook for 1 minute.

2. Gradually whisk in broth, half-and-half, salt, and pepper; bring to a boil. Add pasta; reduce heat to medium. Cover and cook for 12 minutes.

3. Remove from heat; stir in chard leaves until wilted. Garnish with pepper, if desired.

CHICKEN MEATBALL SKILLET SUPPER

MAKES 4 TO 6 SERVINGS

Bright, fresh flavors shine in this easy dish.

- 1 (16-ounce) package ground chicken
- ¼ cup finely chopped yellow onion
- 2 tablespoons minced garlic, divided
- ⅓ cup plain dried bread crumbs
- 3 tablespoons whole milk
- ¼ cup chopped fresh parsley
- 1 teaspoon chopped fresh oregano
- 1 large egg, lightly beaten
- ½ teaspoon kosher salt
- 1 lemon, thinly sliced
- 2 tablespoons unsalted butter
- 2 teaspoons fresh oregano
- 1 cup uncooked orzo pasta
- 3 cups less-sodium chicken broth
- ½ (5-ounce) container fresh baby spinach
- 3 ounces crumbled feta cheese

Garnish: fresh oregano

1. Preheat oven to 400°.

2. In a medium bowl, combine chicken, onion, 1 tablespoon garlic, bread crumbs, milk, parsley, oregano, egg, and salt. Using your hands, gently combine mixture. Be careful not to overmix. Using a 1-tablespoon scoop, scoop mixture and shape into 2-tablespoon balls (about 36 balls).

3. In a 12-inch enameled cast-iron skillet, cook chicken meatballs over medium-high heat until browned. Remove from skillet.

4. In same skillet, add sliced lemon, spreading slices out, and cook over medium-high heat until browned on each side. Remove from skillet.

5. In same skillet, melt butter over medium-high heat. Add remaining 1 tablespoon garlic, oregano, and pasta; cook until aromatic, about 1 minute. Add broth, scraping bottom of pan to loosen any browned bits. Add chicken meatballs and lemon slices.

6. Bake until pasta is al dente, 25 to 30 minutes. There still will be liquid in the skillet. Remove from oven. Stir in spinach; cover and let stand for 10 minutes. Sprinkle with feta cheese. Garnish with oregano, if desired.

ROSEMARY CHICKEN POT PIE

MAKES 1 (10-INCH) PIE

You can't go wrong with this classic combination.

- 2 pounds bone-in skin-on chicken breasts
- 1⅓ tablespoons canola oil
- 1½ tablespoons plus 1 teaspoon kosher salt, divided
- 1½ teaspoons ground black pepper, divided
- 8 tablespoons unsalted butter, softened and divided
- 1 cup chopped peeled parsnip
- 1 cup chopped fennel bulb
- ¼ cup diced red onion
- 1 cup chopped leek (white and light green parts only)
- 2 cloves garlic, minced
- 2½ cups chicken stock
- 1 cup (½-inch) cubed red potatoes
- ⅓ cup all-purpose flour
- ½ cup heavy whipping cream
- 1½ tablespoons minced fresh rosemary
- 1½ tablespoons dry sherry
- 1½ (14.1-ounce) packages refrigerated piecrusts
- 1 large egg white, lightly beaten

1. Preheat oven to 425°.

2. Line a baking sheet with parchment paper.

3. Pat chicken dry, and place on prepared pan. Rub chicken with oil, and sprinkle with 1 teaspoon salt and ½ teaspoon pepper.

4. Roast until a meat thermometer inserted in thickest portion registers 165°, 30 to 35 minutes. Let cool for 20 minutes. Discard skin and bones from chicken; shred meat.

5. In a large Dutch oven, heat 2 tablespoons butter over medium heat. Add parsnip, fennel, and onion; cover and cook, stirring occasionally, until almost tender, about 6 minutes. Stir in leek and garlic; cover and cook until leek is softened, about 3 minutes. Stir in stock and potatoes; bring to a boil. Reduce heat to medium-low; cover and simmer, stirring occasionally, until potatoes are almost tender, about 12 minutes.

6. In a small bowl, stir together flour and remaining 6 tablespoons butter until a smooth paste forms; stir into vegetable mixture with cream. Increase heat to medium-high; cook until sauce is thickened, 5 to 8 minutes. Stir in chicken, rosemary, sherry, remaining 1½ tablespoons salt, and remaining 1 teaspoon pepper. Remove from heat, and cover to keep warm.

7. On a lightly floured surface, roll 1 piecrust to ⅛-inch thickness. Using leaf-shaped cutters, cut dough, and place cutouts on a plate; refrigerate until ready to use. Roll second piecrust into a 12-inch circle. Transfer to a 9-inch deep-dish pie plate, pressing into bottom and up sides. Roll third piecrust into a 12-inch circle.

8. Spoon filling into prepared crust; cover with remaining rolled crust. Fold edges under, and crimp as desired. Brush top crust with egg white. Cut slits in top of dough to release steam. Decorate with leaf cutouts, and brush leaves with egg white. Place pie on a baking sheet.

9. Bake on lowest oven rack until crust is golden brown and filling is bubbly, 50 minutes to 1 hour and 5 minutes, covering with foil after 20 minutes of baking to prevent excess browning. Let cool for 20 minutes before slicing.

PASTA LIMONE

MAKES 6 SERVINGS

This cheesy, lemon-herb pasta will leave you feeling light thanks to tangy goat cheese and zesty lemon.

- 1 (32-ounce) container vegetable stock
- 3 sprigs fresh basil
- 2 cloves garlic, thinly sliced
- 1 large lemon, zested and juiced (see Kitchen Tip)
- 1 teaspoon kosher salt
- ¾ teaspoon ground black pepper
- 1 (16-ounce) package gemelli pasta
- 1 cup grated Parmesan cheese
- ½ cup crumbled goat cheese
- 2 cups fresh baby arugula
- Garnish: lemon zest, crumbled goat cheese

1. In a 12-inch enameled cast-iron skillet, bring stock, basil, garlic, lemon zest, salt, and pepper to a boil over medium-high heat. Add pasta; cover and cook for 10 minutes.

2. Discard basil. Add lemon juice, Parmesan, and goat cheese. Stir in arugula. Garnish with lemon zest and goat cheese, if desired.

KITCHEN TIP Don't pass on the freshly squeezed lemon juice. Since the vitamin C in juice loses its potency over time, freshly squeezed juice really makes all the difference.

SIDES

chapter 4

BRAISED CABBAGE WEDGES

MAKES 6 SERVINGS

This isn't your grandma's braised cabbage. Searing the wedges before simmering them in a spiced sauce imparts layers of flavor and makes the veggie meltingly tender.

- **6 tablespoons olive oil, divided**
- **1 medium head green cabbage, cut into 8 wedges**
- **1½ teaspoons kosher salt, divided**
- **1 teaspoon ground black pepper, divided**
- **4 cloves garlic, minced**
- **1½ teaspoons ground coriander**
- **¼ cup tomato paste**
- **2 cups vegetable broth**

Garnish: crushed red pepper

1. Preheat oven to 350°.

2. In a 12-inch cast-iron skillet, heat 4 tablespoons oil over medium heat. Add cabbage; cook until browned on each side, 3 to 5 minutes. Remove cabbage from skillet; sprinkle with ½ teaspoon salt and ½ teaspoon black pepper.

3. Add remaining 2 tablespoons olive oil, garlic, coriander, remaining 1 teaspoon salt, and remaining ½ teaspoon black pepper to skillet; cook over medium heat, stirring occasionally, until oil begins to sizzle, about 2 minutes. Add tomato paste; cook, stirring frequently, until mixture begins to slightly darken, 1 to 2 minutes. Stir in broth until smooth; return cabbage to skillet. Bring to a boil over medium-high heat.

4. Bake until cabbage is soft and liquid has slightly reduced, 40 to 45 minutes. Garnish with red pepper, if desired.

ROASTED CAULIFLOWER WITH SMOKED PAPRIKA

MAKES 6 TO 8 SERVINGS

Paprika adds smoky flavor to this simple skillet-roasted side.

- **1 head cauliflower, cut into large florets**
- **2 tablespoons chopped fresh thyme**
- **2 teaspoons kosher salt**
- **⅓ cup unsalted butter, melted**
- **1½ teaspoons smoked paprika**
- **Garnish: ground black pepper, chopped fresh thyme**

1. Preheat oven to 425°.
2. In a 12-inch cast-iron skillet, stir together cauliflower, thyme, and salt.
3. In a small bowl, stir together melted butter and paprika; let stand for 3 minutes. Drizzle butter mixture over cauliflower mixture, stirring to coat.
4. Bake until tender, about 25 minutes. Increase oven to broil. Broil until browned, 6 to 8 minutes more. Garnish with pepper and thyme, if desired.

CREAMY ROASTED CAULIFLOWER

MAKES 6 TO 8 SERVINGS

Rich and packed with a flavorful bite, these veggies will become a frequent suppertime side.

- 2 heads cauliflower (about 2 pounds each), cut into florets
- 2 leeks, cut in half and thinly sliced (white parts only)
- 2 tablespoons olive oil
- 2 teaspoons kosher salt, divided
- 1 teaspoon ground black pepper
- 3 tablespoons unsalted butter
- 4 cloves garlic, chopped
- 2 teaspoons fresh thyme leaves
- 3 tablespoons all-purpose flour
- 2½ cups whole milk
- 1 (8-ounce) block sharp white Cheddar cheese, shredded

Garnish: fresh thyme

1. Preheat oven to 450°.
2. On a rimmed baking sheet, toss together cauliflower, leeks, oil, 1 teaspoon salt, and pepper.
3. Bake until browned, 30 to 40 minutes, stirring occasionally. Spoon into a 10-inch cast-iron skillet. Increase oven temperature to broil.
4. In a medium saucepan, melt butter over medium heat. Add garlic and thyme; cook, stirring constantly, for 1 minute. Add flour; cook, stirring frequently, for 1 minute. Gradually whisk in milk and remaining 1 teaspoon salt. Cook, stirring frequently, until thickened and bubbly, 4 to 5 minutes. Remove from heat, and stir in cheese until melted. Pour cheese mixture over cauliflower.
5. Broil about 8 inches from heat until browned, 6 to 8 minutes. Garnish with thyme, If desired.

LODGE

ROASTED GREEN BEANS

MAKES 6 TO 8 SERVINGS

We swapped the baking dish for a sheet pan to give this side dish hearty classic flavor.

- 2 pounds fresh or thawed frozen green beans, trimmed
- 1 large red onion, sliced (about ¾ pound)
- 1 (8-ounce) package sliced fresh baby portobello mushrooms
- 4 slices center-cut bacon, chopped
- ¼ cup canola oil
- 2¼ teaspoons kosher salt
- ¾ teaspoon ground black pepper
- 1 tablespoon chopped fresh thyme
- 1 tablespoon apple cider vinegar
- 1 cup crumbled pork rinds

1. Preheat oven to 425°.
2. Line a large baking sheet with parchment paper.
3. Spread beans, onion, mushrooms, and bacon on prepared pan so they fit in a single layer. (Use two baking sheets, if necessary.) Drizzle with oil, and sprinkle with salt and pepper, tossing to coat.
4. Bake until vegetables are browned and tender, 30 to 35 minutes. Transfer vegetables to a single baking sheet or desired serving dish. Add thyme and vinegar, tossing to coat. Top with pork rinds. Serve immediately.

HASSELBACK BUTTERNUT SQUASH WITH CANE SYRUP GLAZE

MAKES 6 TO 8 SERVINGS

This showstopping side is covered with a sweet and spicy syrup.

- 1 large butternut squash, peeled, halved, and seeded
- 1 tablespoon extra-virgin olive oil
- 1 teaspoon kosher salt
- ½ teaspoon ground black pepper
- 2 tablespoons unsalted butter
- ¼ cup cane syrup
- ¼ cup roughly chopped pecans
- ¼ teaspoon ground ginger
- ¼ teaspoon crushed red pepper

1. Preheat oven to 425°.
2. In a 12-inch cast-iron skillet, place squash cut side down. Brush with oil, and sprinkle with salt and black pepper.
3. Bake for 30 minutes. Let cool for 5 minutes. Remove from skillet; carefully slice squash at ¼-inch intervals, cutting three-fourths of the way through (see Kitchen Tip). Return to skillet; bake 10 minutes more.
4. In a small saucepan, melt butter over medium heat. Add cane syrup, pecans, ginger, and red pepper; bring to a boil. Remove from heat; let stand until slightly thickened, about 3 minutes. Spoon glaze over squash; bake until fork-tender, about 10 minutes more.

KITCHEN TIP Place two wooden chopsticks on either side of squash before slicing to prevent the knife from cutting all the way through.

GRILLED SQUASH GRATINS

MAKES 6 SERVINGS

These personalized portions of smoky veggies with a crunchy, golden-brown topping make a great light lunch or supper side.

- 6 cups (¼-inch-thick) sliced yellow squash
- 6 cups (¼-inch-thick) sliced zucchini
- 1 large red onion, cut into ½-inch-thick rings
- ¼ cup olive oil
- 1 tablespoon kosher salt
- 2 teaspoons ground black pepper
- 1 cup seasoned panko (Japanese bread crumbs)
- 1 cup shredded Parmesan cheese
- ¼ cup chopped fresh chives
- 1 tablespoon chopped fresh thyme
- 1 teaspoon garlic powder
- 2 tablespoons unsalted butter, melted

Garnish: chopped fresh chives

1. Heat a cast-iron grill pan over medium-high heat. In a large bowl, stir together squash, zucchini, onion, olive oil, salt, and pepper until well combined. Grill vegetables in batches until lightly browned, 1 to 2 minutes per side.

2. Preheat oven to 350°. Spray 6 (5-inch) square cast-iron baking dishes with cooking spray.

3. In a medium bowl, stir together bread crumbs, cheese, chives, thyme, garlic powder, and melted butter until well combined.

4. In each dish, place a single layer of squash and zucchini. Top with a few onion slices, and sprinkle with about 1½ tablespoons bread crumb mixture. Repeat layers to use all ingredients.

5. Bake for 20 minutes. Rotate dishes in oven; bake until golden brown, 10 to 12 minutes more. Let stand for 10 minutes before serving. Garnish with chives, if desired.

BUTTERNUT SQUASH WITH HONEY-BUTTER BENNE

MAKES 4 TO 6 SERVINGS

Toasting the benne seeds enhances their nutty flavor and crunch, making them the ideal topping for this sweet side dish.

- **¼ cup benne seeds**
- **4 cups (1½-inch pieces) chopped peeled butternut squash (about 1 large squash)**
- **1 cup thinly sliced yellow onion**
- **2 tablespoons olive oil**
- **1 tablespoon chopped fresh sage**
- **1½ teaspoons kosher salt, divided**
- **1 teaspoon ground ginger**
- **1 teaspoon garlic powder**
- **½ teaspoon ground black pepper**
- **2 tablespoons unsalted butter**
- **2 tablespoons honey**

Garnish: fresh sage

1. Preheat oven to 400°.
2. Place benne in a 12-inch cast-iron skillet, and place skillet in oven while oven heats. Bake until benne seeds are lightly browned and fragrant, about 5 minutes. Remove seeds from skillet.
3. Meanwhile, in a large bowl, stir together squash, onion, oil, chopped sage, 1 teaspoon salt, ginger, garlic powder, and pepper until well combined. Transfer squash mixture to heated skillet.
4. Bake, stirring vegetables every 10 minutes, until squash is tender, about 30 minutes.
5. Remove from oven; stir toasted benne, butter, honey, and remaining ½ teaspoon salt into vegetables. Garnish with sage, if desired. Serve immediately.

MINI SALTED BAKED POTATOES WITH SCALLION SOUR CREAM

MAKES 8 SERVINGS

A classic baked potato is made even more delicious with a delightfully salty crust and an indulgent dollop of sour cream.

FOR POTATOES
16 (2- to 3-inch) Yukon gold potatoes (about 3 pounds)
2 tablespoons olive oil
1½ to 2 cups kosher salt
¼ cup unsalted butter, cut into 16 cubes
Scallion Sour Cream (recipe follows)
Garnish: green onion curls

FOR SCALLION SOUR CREAM
1 cup sour cream
3 scallions, finely minced
2 tablespoons minced fresh parsley
1 tablespoon Dijon mustard
Kosher salt and ground black pepper, to taste

FOR POTATOES

1. Preheat oven to 400°.
2. Wash and dry potatoes. Poke a few holes in each potato with a fork. Rub potatoes with oil, and arrange in a baking pan. Sprinkle salt over potatoes.
3. Bake until tender when pierced with a fork, 45 to 55 minutes.
4. Carefully remove warm potatoes from salt, lightly dusting off some of salt. Arrange on a serving plate, and split open with a fork. Add a butter cube to each potato. Dollop each potato with Scallion Sour Cream. Garnish with green onion, if desired. Serve warm.

FOR SCALLION SOUR CREAM

1. In a small bowl, stir together sour cream, scallions, parsley, and mustard. Season with salt and pepper. Cover and refrigerate for up to 2 days.

SORGHUM AND CHILI ROASTED POTATO WEDGES

MAKES 4 TO 6 SERVINGS

Tender with a sweet and spicy glaze, these potatoes will be a frequent visitor at the table throughout the year.

- **3 tablespoons olive oil**
- **2 tablespoons sorghum syrup**
- **1 tablespoon apple cider vinegar**
- **1½ teaspoons kosher salt**
- **1 teaspoon stone-ground mustard**
- **1 teaspoon chili powder**
- **3 medium russet potatoes, cut into wedges**
- **1 small jalapeño, sliced**

Garnish: sorghum syrup, coarse sea salt

1. Preheat oven to 425°.
2. In a large bowl, whisk together oil, sorghum syrup, vinegar, salt, mustard, and chili powder until combined. Stir in potatoes and jalapeño until coated. Place in an even layer on a cast-iron baking sheet.
3. Bake until tender, about 30 minutes, stirring halfway through. Garnish with sorghum syrup and sea salt, if desired.

POTATOES AU GRATIN WITH GRUYÈRE

MAKES ABOUT 6 SERVINGS

Thinly sliced potatoes soak up the rich and creamy cheese sauce as they simmer in the oven.

- 3 tablespoons unsalted butter
- 2 cloves garlic, minced
- 3 tablespoons all-purpose flour
- 2 teaspoons kosher salt
- 1 teaspoon ground cumin
- ¼ teaspoon ground black pepper
- 2 cups whole milk
- 1½ cups shredded Gruyère cheese, divided
- 1 tablespoon chopped fresh thyme
- 2 large russet potatoes, thinly sliced (about 5 cups)

Garnish: chopped fresh thyme

1. Preheat oven to 350°.
2. Spray a 9-inch square baking pan with cooking spray. Place pan on a large rimmed baking sheet.
3. In a small saucepan, melt butter over medium heat. Whisk in garlic, flour, salt, cumin, and pepper until smooth; cook, stirring constantly, until bubbly, about 3 minutes. Gradually add milk, whisking until smooth; bring to a boil. Cook until thickened, about 2 minutes. Remove from heat; add 1 cup cheese and thyme, stirring until cheese is melted. Layer potatoes in prepared pan. Pour cheese mixture over potatoes. Sprinkle with remaining ½ cup cheese. Cover with foil.
4. Bake for 1 hour. Uncover and bake until potatoes are tender and golden brown, 30 to 35 minutes more. Let cool for 5 minutes. Garnish with thyme, if desired.

BROWNED BUTTER MASHED POTATOES

MAKES 6 SERVINGS

We chose Yukon gold potatoes for this rich side dish because they're smooth when mashed without any graininess.

- 2 pounds Yukon gold potatoes, peeled and diced
- 5 teaspoons kosher salt, divided
- 6 tablespoons unsalted butter
- ¾ cup heavy whipping cream, room temperature
- 1½ teaspoons chopped fresh sage
- ¾ teaspoon ground black pepper
- ½ teaspoon garlic powder
- ½ teaspoon ground nutmeg

Garnish: fresh sage

1. In a large Dutch oven, bring potatoes, 3 teaspoons salt, and water to cover by 2 inches to a boil over medium-high heat. Cook until tender, about 20 minutes. Drain well.

2. In a small cast-iron skillet, cook butter over medium heat, swirling pan occasionally, until it turns a medium-brown color and has a nutty aroma, about 8 minutes. Remove from heat; strain through a fine-mesh sieve, reserving butter and discarding solids.

3. In a large bowl, combine potatoes, half of browned butter, cream, sage, pepper, garlic powder, nutmeg, and remaining 2 teaspoons salt, mashing with a potato masher until smooth. Top with remaining browned butter. Garnish with sage, if desired.

CREAMED SPINACH MASHED POTATOES

MAKES 6 TO 8 SERVINGS

This dish combines two classic meals in one, creating a new go-to side everyone will love.

- 2 pounds Yukon gold potatoes
- 1½ cups heavy whipping cream, divided
- 1 tablespoon plus 2 teaspoons kosher salt, divided
- 3 tablespoons unsalted butter
- 1 cup chopped yellow onion
- 2 cloves garlic, chopped
- 2 (9-ounce) bags fresh spinach
- 1 cup shredded Gouda cheese
- ½ cup freshly grated Parmesan cheese

1. Preheat oven to 400°. Place a wire rack on center oven rack.
2. Wrap potatoes in foil, and place on wire rack.
3. Bake until fork-tender, about 1 hour. Let stand for 5 minutes.
4. Carefully peel potatoes. In a large bowl, mash potatoes with a potato ricer or masher until smooth; stir in 1 cup cream and 1 tablespoon salt.
5. In a large cast-iron skillet, melt butter over medium heat. Add onion and garlic; cook, stirring occasionally, until onion becomes translucent, 3 to 4 minutes. Increase heat to medium-high. Working in batches, add spinach, and cook, stirring frequently, until spinach is wilted, 3 to 4 minutes per batch. Cook, stirring frequently, until liquid is evaporated, 3 to 4 minutes. Stir in remaining ½ cup cream and remaining 2 teaspoons salt. Remove from skillet, and wipe skillet clean.
6. Spoon mashed potatoes into same skillet. Cook over medium heat, stirring occasionally, until hot, 2 to 3 minutes. Remove from heat. Stir in cheeses. Swirl in spinach mixture. Serve warm.

CREAMY PECAN-STUFFED SWEET POTATOES

MAKES 4 SERVINGS

Sort of like a deconstructed, sweet, and spicy homage to Southerners' well-loved sweet potato casserole, this sensational side will pleasantly surprise anyone you serve it to.

- 4 medium sweet potatoes, scrubbed well and pricked all over with a fork
- 1 tablespoon olive oil
- 1¼ teaspoons kosher salt, divided
- 3 ounces cream cheese, softened
- ¼ cup unsalted butter, softened
- 2 tablespoons firmly packed light brown sugar
- ¾ teaspoon chili powder
- ½ teaspoon ground cinnamon
- ½ cup plus 2 tablespoons finely chopped pecans, divided
- Cane or sorghum syrup, for drizzling

1. Preheat oven to 425°.
2. Rub potatoes with oil; sprinkle with 1 teaspoon salt. Place potatoes in a 10-inch cast-iron skillet.
3. Bake until potatoes are easily pierced with a fork, 45 to 55 minutes. Remove potatoes from skillet, and let cool enough to handle. Reduce oven temperature to 350°.
4. In a small bowl, stir together cream cheese, butter, brown sugar, chili powder, cinnamon, and remaining ¼ teaspoon salt until smooth; stir in ½ cup pecans.
5. Split potatoes lengthwise; gently fluff flesh with a fork. Divide cream cheese mixture among potatoes; return potatoes to skillet.
6. Bake until filling is lightly browned, 15 to 20 minutes. Drizzle with syrup, and sprinkle with remaining 2 tablespoons pecans. Serve immediately.

SMOKY SWEET POTATO GRATIN CASSEROLE

MAKES 6 TO 8 SERVINGS

Chipotle peppers are the secret to this comfort-made casserole.

- 2 teaspoons unsalted butter
- 2 cups heavy whipping cream
- 3 cloves garlic, crushed
- 2 to 3 teaspoons fresh thyme leaves
- 3½ teaspoons kosher salt, divided
- ½ teaspoon smoked paprika
- ½ teaspoon ground black pepper, divided
- ⅛ teaspoon ground nutmeg
- 1 tablespoon finely chopped chipotle peppers in adobo sauce
- 3 pounds sweet potatoes, peeled and thinly sliced
- ½ cup shredded Parmesan cheese
- Garnish: chopped fresh thyme

1. Preheat oven to 325°.

2. Grease a shallow 11x8-inch baking dish with butter.

3. In a medium saucepan, bring cream, garlic, thyme leaves, 2 teaspoons salt, paprika, ¼ teaspoon black pepper, and nutmeg to a gentle boil over medium heat. Reduce heat to low; simmer until garlic is tender, about 15 minutes. Remove from heat, and stir in chipotle peppers.

4. In a large bowl, combine potatoes, remaining 1½ teaspoons salt, and remaining ¼ teaspoon black pepper. Layer potatoes in prepared pan. Pour cream mixture over potatoes. Tightly cover with foil.

5. Bake until potatoes are tender, 1 hour and 30 minutes to 2 hours. Uncover and top with cheese. Bake until cheese is melted, about 15 minutes more. Garnish with chopped thyme, if desired.

CHARRED BABY CARROTS

MAKES 6 SERVINGS

Perfectly blistered and lightly spiced, these carrots are also an excellent pairing for grilled chicken or cooked grains.

- **3 tablespoons unsalted butter**
- **2 pounds baby carrots, peeled and trimmed**
- **2 cloves garlic, smashed**
- **1½ teaspoons kosher salt**
- **1 teaspoon ground black pepper**
- **½ teaspoon ground cardamom**
- **2 tablespoons chopped fresh parsley**

Garnish: chopped fresh parsley

1. In a large cast-iron skillet, melt butter over medium-high heat. Add carrots, garlic, salt, pepper, and cardamom; cover and cook, stirring occasionally, until charred and tender, about 15 minutes.

2. Stir in 2 tablespoons parsley. Garnish with additional parsley, if desired.

GLAZED BACON-WRAPPED CARROTS

MAKES 4 TO 6 SERVINGS

For an eye-catching side dish or appetizer, try your hand at these beauties. They deliver everything you'd want in one bite—sweetness, saltiness, and a touch of spice.

10 slices thick-cut bacon
10 medium carrots with tops, peeled and trimmed
¼ cup honey
1½ teaspoons hot sauce
½ teaspoon smoked paprika
⅛ teaspoon crushed red pepper
Garnish: chopped fresh parsley

1. Preheat oven to 400°.
2. Wrap 1 slice bacon around each carrot. Place on a large cast-iron baking sheet.
3. Bake until bacon begins to crisp, 25 to 30 minutes.
4. In a small bowl, whisk together honey, hot sauce, paprika, and red pepper; brush onto bacon.
5. Bake until bacon is golden brown and crisp, 15 to 20 minutes more. Brush with remaining honey mixture. Garnish with parsley, if desired.

KITCHEN TIP This technique also works great with parsnips, asparagus, and green bean bundles.

GRILLED BABY ONIONS WITH CRUNCHY HERBED RICE

MAKES 6 SERVINGS

An herbaceous lemon dressing brings together sweet grilled onions and buttery rice for an impressive side dish to rival any main.

- 8 cups water
- 2 cups long-grain white rice
- 4¾ teaspoons kosher salt, divided
- 1 teaspoon garlic powder
- ¾ teaspoon ground black pepper, divided
- ½ teaspoon ground cumin
- ¼ cup unsalted butter
- ½ cup plus 2 tablespoons chopped fresh parsley, divided
- 1 pound baby sweet onions, with green tops attached, halved lengthwise if large
- ½ cup plus 2 teaspoons olive oil, divided
- 1 teaspoon lemon zest
- 2 tablespoons fresh lemon juice
- 3 cloves garlic, grated
- ¼ teaspoon crushed red pepper

Garnish: lemon zest

1. In a medium cast-iron Dutch oven, bring 8 cups water to a boil over medium-high heat. Stir in rice and 2 teaspoons salt. Cook, stirring occasionally, until rice is just tender, 10 to 12 minutes. Drain well; spread rice in an even layer on a parchment paper-lined baking sheet. Let cool completely.

2. Sprinkle 1 teaspoon salt, garlic powder, ½ teaspoon black pepper, and cumin onto rice; stir until combined.

3. In a 12-inch cast-iron skillet with lid, heat butter over medium heat until bubbly. Spoon rice into skillet, pressing to an even layer. Cover surface of rice with a piece of parchment paper; cover with lid. Reduce heat to medium-low. Cook until rice is lightly browned on bottom, 40 to 45 minutes, increasing heat to medium, if needed. Using a spatula, scrape and stir browned bits from bottom of skillet into rice. Stir in 2 tablespoons parsley.

4. Meanwhile, heat a cast-iron grill pan over medium-high heat. On a rimmed baking sheet, toss together onion, 2 teaspoons oil, ½ teaspoon salt, and remaining ¼ teaspoon black pepper. Grill onions until browned and tender, 3 to 4 minutes per side.

5. In a medium bowl, whisk together lemon zest and juice, grated garlic, red pepper, remaining 1¼ teaspoons salt, and remaining ½ cup parsley; slowly whisk in remaining ½ cup oil until well combined.

6. Top rice with grilled onion, and drizzle with lemon dressing. Garnish with zest, if desired.

GREEK VEGETABLE CRISP

MAKES 8 TO 10 SERVINGS

Crisps aren't just for dessert. This Mediterranean-inspired side features a bevy of colorful produce topped with a savory, buttery oat crumble.

- ¾ cup all-purpose flour
- ½ cup old-fashioned oats
- 1 tablespoon light brown sugar
- 2 teaspoons kosher salt, divided
- ⅓ cup unsalted butter, melted
- 6 cloves garlic, minced and divided
- 2 tablespoons unsalted butter
- 1 bulb fennel, thinly sliced and fronds reserved for garnish
- ½ cup dry white wine
- 3 cups (½-inch) chopped Yukon gold potatoes (about 4 medium)
- 2 cups (½-inch) chopped zucchini (about 1 large)
- 2 cups (½-inch) chopped peeled eggplant (about 1 small)
- 1 (28-ounce) can peeled whole tomatoes, drained, liquid reserved, and roughly chopped
- 1 (6.5-ounce) jar pitted kalamata olives, drained

Garnish: feta cheese

1. Preheat oven to 350°.

2. In a small bowl, whisk together flour, oats, brown sugar, and 1 teaspoon salt. Stir in melted butter and 2 cloves minced garlic until large crumbs form. Cover and refrigerate.

3. In a 12-inch cast-iron skillet, melt butter over medium heat. Add fennel, remaining 4 cloves minced garlic, and remaining 1 teaspoon salt; cook, stirring occasionally, until fennel is just soft, about 6 minutes. Add wine; cook, stirring occasionally, for 2 minutes. Stir in potatoes, zucchini, eggplant, tomatoes, tomato liquid, and olives.

4. Bake for 30 minutes. Stir vegetables; sprinkle oat mixture onto vegetables.

5. Bake until topping is golden brown, liquid has slightly reduced, and vegetables are tender, 30 to 40 minutes more. Let stand for 10 minutes before serving. Garnish with feta and reserved fennel fronds, if desired.

ROASTED VEGETABLE RICE

MAKES 6 TO 8 SERVINGS

This bountiful side dish is the perfect blend of fresh vegetables and savory flavors.

- 4 slices thick-cut bacon, cut into 1-inch pieces
- 2½ cups plus 2 tablespoons vegetable broth
- 1½ cups wild blend rice*
- 3 teaspoons kosher salt, divided
- 1 pound Brussels sprouts, trimmed and halved
- 4 large carrots, peeled and sliced
- ½ red onion, sliced
- 1 red bell pepper, cut into 1-inch pieces
- 5 tablespoons olive oil, divided
- ¼ cup balsamic vinegar
- 3 tablespoons firmly packed light brown sugar
- 2 tablespoons molasses
- 1 teaspoon fresh thyme leaves
- ½ teaspoon ground black pepper
- ½ cup chopped toasted pecans
- ¼ cup chopped fresh parsley

Garnish: chopped fresh parsley, toasted pecans

1. Preheat oven to 425°.
2. On a rimmed baking sheet, place bacon.
3. Bake until almost crispy, about 8 minutes. Leave oven on.
4. In a medium saucepan, combine broth, rice, and 1 teaspoon salt, and bring to a boil over medium heat. Cover, reduce heat, and simmer until broth is absorbed and rice is tender, 35 to 45 minutes. Remove from heat. Let stand for 10 minutes. Fluff rice with a fork.
5. On rimmed baking sheet with bacon, toss together Brussels sprouts, carrots, red onion, bell pepper, 2 tablespoons oil, and 1 teaspoon salt.
6. Bake until sprouts are roasted, about 20 minutes, stirring halfway through baking.
7. In small bowl, whisk together vinegar, brown sugar, molasses, thyme, black pepper, remaining 3 tablespoons oil, and remaining 1 teaspoon salt. Add to warm vegetables, tossing to coat.
8. In desired serving bowl, stir together rice, vegetable mixture, pecans, and parsley. Garnish with parsley and pecans, if desired.

**We used Lundberg Wild Blend Rice.*

EXTRA-CHEESY MACARONI AND CHEESE

MAKES 8 TO 10 SERVINGS

Serve this mac and cheese hot and bubbling right out of the oven.

- ¼ cup unsalted butter
- ¼ cup all-purpose flour
- 2½ cups whole milk
- 1½ teaspoons dry mustard
- 1 teaspoon kosher salt
- ½ teaspoon ground black pepper
- ¼ teaspoon ground nutmeg
- 6 ounces processed cheese product,* cubed
- 1¼ cups shredded sharp Cheddar cheese, divided
- 1 pound elbow macaroni, cooked according to package directions

1. Preheat oven to broil.
2. In a 12-inch cast-iron skillet, melt butter over medium-low heat. Whisk in flour; cook, stirring constantly, until bubbly, about 3 minutes. Gradually whisk in milk until smooth. Add mustard, salt, pepper, and nutmeg; cook, stirring frequently, until thickened, about 5 minutes. Stir in cheese product and 1 cup Cheddar until melted. Remove from heat; add cooked pasta, stirring until combined. Sprinkle with remaining ¼ cup Cheddar.
3. Broil until golden brown and bubbly, about 5 minutes.

**We used Velveeta.*

DESSERTS

chapter 5

CINNAMON HOT CHOCOLATE DOUGHNUTS

MAKES 17 TO 19

Bring the pastry shop to your home with these chocolate-filled, cinnamon-sugar-coated delights.

FOR DOUGHNUTS

- 4½ cups all-purpose flour
- 2 cups sugar, divided
- 1½ tablespoons active dry yeast
- 1¼ teaspoons kosher salt
- 2 large eggs
- 1¼ cups warm whole milk (105° to 110°)
- ¼ cup warm water (105° to 110°)
- ¼ cup unsalted butter, softened
- 4 cups vegetable oil, for frying
- 2 tablespoons ground cinnamon
- Hot Chocolate Filling (recipe follows)

FOR HOT CHOCOLATE FILLING

- 8 ounces bittersweet chocolate, finely chopped
- ¾ cup heavy whipping cream
- 2 tablespoons drinking chocolate

FOR DOUGHNUTS

1. In the bowl of a stand mixer fitted with the paddle attachment, combine flour, 1 cup sugar, yeast, and salt. Stir in eggs. With mixer at low speed, gradually add warm milk and ¼ cup warm water, beating until dough comes together. Increase mixer speed to medium-high, and beat for 5 to 7 minutes.

2. Switch to the dough hook attachment. With mixer at medium-high speed, add butter, 1 tablespoon at a time, letting each piece fully incorporate before adding the next. Beat until a smooth dough forms, about 3 minutes. (Dough will be sticky.)

3. Spray a large bowl with cooking spray. Place dough in bowl, turning to grease top. Cover and let rise in a warm, draft-free place (75°) until doubled in size, 1 hour and 30 minutes to 2 hours.

4. Turn out dough onto a heavily floured surface, and gently pat to ½-inch thickness. Using a 2½-inch round cutter, cut dough. Loosely cover with plastic wrap, and let rise until doubled in size, about 1 hour and 30 minutes.

5. In a large saucepan or Dutch oven, heat oil over medium heat until a deep-fry thermometer registers 350°. Working in batches, fry doughnuts until golden brown, about 1 minute per side. Remove from oil, and let drain on a wire rack.

6. In a small bowl, stir together cinnamon and remaining 1 cup sugar. Toss doughnuts in cinnamon sugar while still warm. Let cool completely.

7. Cut a small X in one side of each doughnut. Place Hot Chocolate Filling in a piping bag fitted with a large round tip, or a resealable plastic bag with 1 corner cut off. Insert tip into X to fill doughnuts. Serve immediately.

FOR HOT CHOCOLATE FILLING

1. Place chopped chocolate in a medium microwave-safe bowl. In a saucepan, whisk together cream and drinking chocolate until well combined. Heat over medium heat, stirring frequently, just until bubbles form around edges of pan. (Do not boil.)

2. Pour hot cream mixture over chocolate; let stand for 1 minute. Using a spatula, begin to stir mixture until smooth. If some chocolate pieces have a hard time melting, place bowl in microwave and heat on high for 10 seconds; stir until smooth. Let cool for 30 minutes.

CLASSIC CINNAMON ROLLS

MAKES 10

Slathered with a tart buttermilk glaze, these tender cinnamon rolls are worth waking up for.

FOR DOUGH

- ¼ cup warm water (105° to 110°)
- 1 (0.25-ounce) package active dry yeast
- 3½ cups all-purpose flour
- ¼ cup granulated sugar
- 1½ teaspoons kosher salt
- ¾ cup whole buttermilk
- 1 large egg, lightly beaten
- 6 tablespoons unsalted butter, softened

FOR FILLING

- ½ cup unsalted butter, softened
- ¾ cup firmly packed light brown sugar
- 2 tablespoons ground cinnamon

FOR GLAZE

- ¼ cup whole buttermilk
- 2 ounces cream cheese, softened
- 2¼ cups confectioners' sugar
- ⅛ teaspoon vanilla extract

FOR DOUGH

1. In a small bowl, stir together ¼ cup warm water and yeast. Let stand until mixture is foamy, about 5 minutes.

2. In the bowl of a stand mixer fitted with the paddle attachment, combine flour, granulated sugar, and salt. With mixer on low speed, add yeast mixture, buttermilk, egg, and butter. Increase mixer speed to medium, and beat until dough comes together. Switch to the dough hook attachment. Beat until dough is smooth and elastic, about 7 minutes.

3. Spray a large bowl with cooking spray. Place dough in bowl, turning to grease top. Cover and let rise in a warm, draft-free place (75°) until doubled in size, about 1 hour and 30 minutes.

4. Lightly punch dough down. On a lightly floured surface, roll dough into a 14x10-inch rectangle.

FOR FILLING

1. Spread butter onto dough. In a small bowl, stir together brown sugar and cinnamon. Sprinkle cinnamon sugar over butter; gently press into dough. Starting with one long side, roll up dough, jelly roll style; pinch seam to seal. Place log, seam side down, and cut into 10 rolls.

2. Spray a 10-inch cast-iron skillet with cooking spray. Place rolls in prepared skillet. Cover and let rise in a warm, draft-free place (75°) until doubled in size, 45 minutes to 1 hour.

3. Preheat oven to 350°.

4. Bake until golden brown, 30 to 35 minutes. Let cool slightly.

FOR GLAZE

1. In a medium bowl, whisk together buttermilk and cream cheese until smooth. Add confectioners' sugar and vanilla; whisk until smooth. Spread glaze onto warm rolls.

CASHEW BANANA BREAD

MAKES 1 (9X5-INCH) LOAF

This modern take on a classic quick bread includes salty, creamy cashews and beautiful sliced bananas nestled on top of the golden-brown loaf.

- ¾ cup sugar
- ¾ cup cashew butter
- ½ cup sour cream
- ¼ cup unsalted butter, melted
- 2 large eggs
- 1 teaspoon vanilla extract
- 1 cup mashed ripe banana (about 3 small bananas)
- 2 cups all-purpose flour
- 1 teaspoon baking powder
- ½ teaspoon baking soda
- ¼ teaspoon kosher salt
- 1 cup chopped cashews
- 1 banana, sliced lengthwise
- 1 tablespoon honey
- Cashew butter, to serve

1. Preheat oven to 350°. Spray a 9x5-inch cast-iron loaf pan with baking spray with flour.
2. In a large bowl, combine sugar, cashew butter, sour cream, melted butter, eggs, and vanilla. Stir in mashed banana.
3. In a medium bowl, whisk together flour, baking powder, baking soda, and salt. Add flour mixture to banana mixture, stirring just until moistened. Stir in cashews. Spoon batter into prepared pan. Top with banana slices.
4. Bake until a wooden pick inserted in center comes out clean, about 2 hours. Brush banana slices with honey. Let cool in pan for 10 minutes. Invert to remove, and let cool completely on a wire rack. Serve with cashew butter.

BACON PEANUT BUTTER COOKIES

MAKES 24

Peanut butter, bacon, and chocolate are a trio sent straight from heaven.

- **½ pound sliced bacon (about 8 to 10 slices)**
- **¼ cup unsalted butter, softened**
- **½ cup firmly packed light brown sugar**
- **½ cup granulated sugar**
- **½ cup creamy peanut butter**
- **1½ teaspoons vanilla extract**
- **1 large egg, room temperature**
- **1¼ cups all-purpose flour**
- **½ teaspoon kosher salt**
- **¼ teaspoon baking soda**
- **¼ teaspoon baking powder**
- **1 cup dark chocolate melting wafers, melted**

1. Preheat oven to 350°.

2. In a large skillet, cook bacon slices over medium-high heat until almost crisp, about 10 minutes. Remove bacon, and let drain on paper towels. Reserve ¼ cup drippings.

3. In a large bowl, beat butter, bacon drippings, and sugars with a mixer at medium speed until fluffy, 3 to 4 minutes, stopping to scrape sides of bowl. Add peanut butter and vanilla, beating until combined. Add egg, beating well.

4. In a medium bowl, whisk together flour, salt, baking soda, and baking powder. With mixer on low speed, gradually add flour mixture to butter mixture, beating just until combined. Crumble bacon, reserving ¼ cup. Stir remaining bacon into batter.

5. Using a 1½-tablespoon scoop, scoop dough, and place 2 inches apart on large rimmed baking sheets. Dip a fork in water, and gently press tines into surface of dough, making a crosshatch design.

6. Bake until light golden brown, about 12 minutes, rotating pans halfway through baking. Let cool on pans for 5 minutes. Remove from pans, and let cool completely on wire racks.

7. Dip cookies halfway into melted chocolate, and place on wire racks. Sprinkle with reserved ¼ cup bacon.

CHOCOLATE CHERRY CHUNK COOKIE

MAKES 6 TO 8 SERVINGS

Inspired by a popular chocolate-cherry ice cream brand, this supersize cookie is chock-full of dried cherries, espresso chocolate chips, and large chunks of white chocolate.

- 1 (5-ounce) bag dried cherries (about 1 cup)
- 1 cup cherry cola, room temperature
- 1 cup unsalted butter, softened
- 1½ cups packed light brown sugar
- 2 large eggs
- 1½ teaspoons vanilla extract
- 2 cups all-purpose flour
- ¼ cup Dutch-process cocoa powder
- 1 teaspoon baking soda
- ¾ teaspoon kosher salt
- 1 (9-ounce) bag espresso chocolate chips
- 1 (4.4-ounce) bar white chocolate, broken into large pieces
- 1 (4-ounce) bar dark chocolate (60% cacao), chopped
- ⅓ cup heavy whipping cream

1. Preheat oven to 350°. Spray a 10-inch cast-iron skillet with baking spray with flour.

2. In a small microwave-safe bowl, combine cherries and cola, and microwave on high for 1 minute. Let stand 10 minutes. Drain.

3. In the bowl of a stand mixer fitted with the paddle attachment, beat butter and brown sugar at medium speed until fluffy, 3 to 4 minutes, stopping to scrape sides of bowl. Reduce mixer speed to medium-low. Add eggs, one at a time, beating well after each addition. Beat in vanilla.

4. In a medium bowl, whisk together flour, cocoa, baking soda, and salt. Reduce mixer speed to low. Gradually add flour mixture to butter mixture, beating just until combined (do not overmix). Gently stir in cherries and espresso chips. Spoon into prepared pan spreading to edges.

5. Bake until edges are browned and center is set but soft, 25 to 30 minutes, or to desired degree of doneness. Remove from oven. While cookie is still hot, place white chocolate pieces on top. Let cool on a wire rack.

6. In a 2-cup glass measuring cup, combine dark chocolate and cream. Microwave on high in 30-second intervals, stirring between each, until chocolate is melted and combined with cream. Drizzle half of dark chocolate mixture over cookie. Serve with remaining dark chocolate mixture.

COCONUT CREAM BARS

MAKES 24

Our semi-no-bake take on the Nanaimo bar, a coconut-and-chocolate treat, features a trifecta of indulgent layers chock-full of nuts and infused with coffee and coconut liqueur.

FOR CRUST
- 1 cup unsalted butter, cubed
- ⅔ cup cocoa powder
- ½ cup granulated sugar
- ⅛ teaspoon kosher salt
- 2 large eggs, lightly beaten
- 3 cups graham cracker crumbs
- 1½ cups sweetened flaked coconut
- 1 cup chopped pecans

FOR FILLING
- 1 cup unsalted butter, softened
- 4 cups confectioners' sugar
- ⅛ teaspoon kosher salt
- 3 tablespoons coconut milk
- 1 tablespoon coconut rum*

FOR TOPPING
- 8 ounces semisweet chocolate, chopped
- 3 tablespoons heavy whipping cream
- 1½ tablespoons coconut oil
- 1 tablespoon coffee liqueur*

1. Preheat oven to 350°. Line a 13x9-inch cast-iron baking pan with aluminum foil, letting excess extend over sides of pan. Lightly spray with cooking spray.

FOR CRUST

1. In a medium heatproof bowl, combine butter, cocoa, granulated sugar, and salt.
2. In a small Dutch oven, pour water to a depth of 1 inch. Bring to a boil over medium-high heat. Reduce heat to low. Place bowl with cocoa mixture over simmering water; cook, stirring occasionally, until butter is melted. While whisking constantly, add eggs; cook until thick and glossy, whisking constantly, about 2 minutes. Remove from heat. Fold in graham cracker crumbs, coconut, and pecans. Press crust mixture into prepared pan.
3. Bake until dry, 10 to 15 minutes. Let cool completely.

FOR FILLING

1. In the bowl of a stand mixer fitted with a paddle attachment, beat butter at medium speed until smooth. Add confectioners' sugar and salt; beat at medium-high speed until fluffy, stopping to scrape down sides of bowl, 4 to 5 minutes. Add coconut milk and rum; beat until combined. Spread mixture in an even layer on top of crust. Chill until firm, 30 to 45 minutes.

FOR TOPPING

1. In a medium heatproof bowl, combine chocolate, cream, coconut oil, and coffee liqueur. Place bowl over Dutch oven of simmering water; cook, stirring occasionally, until melted and smooth. Pour chocolate mixture over filling and smooth with an offset spatula. Chill until chocolate is hardened, 15 to 20 minutes.
2. Using a hot, dry knife, cut into 24 squares. Serve chilled or at room temperature.

**We used Blue Chair Bay Coconut Rum and Kahlúa.*

MOCHA BROWNIES WITH ESPRESSO SWEET CREAM

MAKES 16

Mocha and espresso team up for each delicious, bittersweet bite in this indulgent brownie.

FOR BROWNIES
- 1 (8-ounce) bar bittersweet chocolate, chopped
- ¾ cup unsalted butter, cubed
- 1 cup granulated sugar
- ¾ cup firmly packed dark brown sugar
- 1¼ cups all-purpose flour
- 3 tablespoons unsweetened cocoa powder, sifted
- 1½ teaspoons instant espresso powder
- ¾ teaspoon kosher salt
- 4 large eggs, room temperature and lightly beaten
- 2 teaspoons vanilla extract
- Espresso Sweet Cream (recipe follows)

FOR ESPRESSO SWEET CREAM
- 1 (8-ounce) package cream cheese, softened
- ½ cup sugar
- 2 teaspoons all-purpose flour
- 1½ teaspoons instant espresso powder
- 1 large egg
- 1½ teaspoons vanilla extract

1. Preheat oven to 325°.

FOR BROWNIES

1. Spray an 8-inch square baking pan with cooking spray. Line pan with parchment paper, letting excess extend over sides of pan.
2. In the top of a double boiler, combine chocolate and butter. Cook over simmering water, stirring occasionally, until melted and smooth. Turn off heat, and whisk in sugars until well combined. (Mixture will not be completely smooth.) Remove from heat, and let cool slightly, 3 to 5 minutes.
3. In a medium bowl, whisk together flour, cocoa, espresso powder, and salt.
4. Slowly add eggs to chocolate mixture, whisking until combined. Whisk in vanilla. Fold in flour mixture just until combined. Spread two-thirds of batter (about 2⅔ cups) into prepared pan. Spoon Espresso Sweet Cream on top of batter, smoothing flat with an offset spatula. Spoon remaining batter in large dollops on top of sweet cream. Using a wooden pick, swirl layers together.
5. Bake until brownie on top is shiny, center is set, and a wooden pick inserted in brownie comes out with a few moist crumbs, 55 minutes to 1 hour and 5 minutes, covering edges with foil after 40 minutes of baking to prevent excess browning. Let cool in pan until firm enough to remove, about 30 minutes. Using excess parchment as handles, remove from pan, and let cool completely on a wire rack. Cut into bars. Refrigerate in an airtight container for up to 6 days. Let come to room temperature before serving.

ESPRESSO SWEET CREAM

1. In a medium bowl, whisk cream cheese until smooth. Add sugar, flour, and espresso powder, and whisk until combined, stopping to scrape sides of bowl. Add egg, whisking well. Whisk in vanilla. Use immediately.

FUDGY CHOCOLATE PEANUT BUTTER BROWNIE SUNDAES

MAKES 6 SERVINGS

It doesn't get much more nostalgically delicious than these irresistible sundaes.

- 1⅓ cups sugar
- 1 cup all-purpose flour
- ⅓ cup unsweetened Dutch process cocoa powder
- ½ teaspoon baking powder
- ¼ teaspoon kosher salt
- ½ cup unsalted butter
- ⅔ cup semisweet chocolate chips, divided
- 2 tablespoons creamy peanut butter
- 2 large eggs, lightly beaten
- 1 teaspoon vanilla extract
- ½ cup mini peanut butter cups
- Vanilla ice cream, to serve
- Garnish: chocolate-covered peanuts, hot fudge, mini peanut butter cups

1. Preheat oven to 325°. Spray a 9x9-inch baking pan with baking spray with flour.
2. In a large bowl, whisk together sugar, flour, cocoa powder, baking powder, and salt until combined.
3. In a medium microwave-safe bowl, combine butter and ⅓ cup chocolate chips; heat on high for 1 minute. Stir until chocolate is melted. Stir in peanut butter. Whisk in eggs and vanilla. Stir chocolate mixture into flour mixture until well combined. Stir in peanut butter cups and remaining ⅓ cup chocolate chips. Pour batter into prepared pan, and smooth to edges with spatula.
4. Bake until a wooden pick inserted in center comes out clean, 45 to 50 minutes. Serve warm with ice cream. Garnish with chocolate-covered peanuts, hot fudge, and mini peanut butter cups, if desired.

SALTED CARAMEL AND CHOCOLATE PECAN PIE

MAKES 1 (9-INCH) PIE

It's hard to improve on a Southern icon, but this pie filled with buttery caramel will have any pecan pie lover asking for a second helping.

FOR PIECRUST

- **1½ cups all-purpose flour**
- **1½ teaspoons sugar**
- **½ teaspoon kosher salt**
- **½ cup cold unsalted butter, cubed**
- **¼ cup ice water**

FOR FILLING

- **2 cups sugar**
- **⅔ cup light corn syrup**
- **⅓ cup water**
- **½ cup unsalted butter, cubed and softened**
- **1 cup heavy whipping cream, room temperature**
- **1 teaspoon kosher salt**
- **3 large eggs**
- **3 ounces semisweet chocolate, chopped**
- **1¾ cups pecan halves**

Garnish: sea salt flakes

FOR PIECRUST

1. In the work bowl of a food processor, place flour, sugar, and salt; pulse until combined. Add cold butter, and pulse until mixture is crumbly. With processor running, add ¼ cup ice water in a slow, steady stream just until dough comes together. (Mixture should appear crumbly, but hold together when pinched.)

2. Turn out dough, and shape into a disk. Wrap tightly in plastic wrap, and refrigerate for at least 30 minutes. (Dough may be refrigerated for up to 3 days or frozen for up to 2 months.)

3. On a lightly floured surface, roll dough into a 12-inch circle. Transfer to a 9-inch pie plate, pressing into bottom and up sides. Trim excess dough to ½ inch beyond edge of plate. Fold edges under, and crimp as desired. Freeze for at least 20 minutes.

FOR FILLING

1. In a large skillet, cook sugar, corn syrup, and ⅓ cup water over medium-high heat, without stirring, until deep honey colored, 8 to 10 minutes. Remove from heat. Add butter, stirring until melted. Gradually stir in cream and kosher salt. Pour mixture into a bowl, and let cool for 30 minutes.

2. Preheat oven to 350°.

3. Add eggs to cooled caramel mixture, whisking to combine. Stir in chocolate and pecans. Pour into prepared crust.

4. Bake until set, 50 to 55 minutes. Let cool for at least 1 hour. Garnish with sea salt, if desired.

CHOCOLATE GANACHE TART

MAKES 1 (9-INCH) TART

From a crispy crust to a creamy filling, layers of decadent chocolate combine for this indulgent dessert.

- 2 cups cream-filled chocolate sandwich cookie crumbs (about 23 sandwich cookies)
- ¼ cup unsalted butter, melted
- ¼ cup plus 2 tablespoons unsweetened cocoa powder, divided
- ½ teaspoon kosher salt
- 2 (3.5-ounce) bars dark chocolate, chopped
- 3 tablespoons ginger preserves
- 1 (13.5-ounce) can premium coconut milk
- ¼ cup sugar
- ¼ cup heavy whipping cream

Garnish: chopped crystallized ginger, toasted flaked coconut, fresh rosemary

1. In a medium bowl, stir together cookie crumbs, melted butter, 2 tablespoons cocoa, and salt until combined. Press crumb mixture into bottom and up sides of a 9-inch round fluted removable-bottom tart pan. Freeze for at least 20 minutes.
2. In the work bowl of a food processor, place chocolate, preserves, and remaining ¼ cup cocoa.
3. In a medium saucepan, cook coconut milk, sugar, and cream over medium-low heat, stirring frequently, until sugar melts and bubbles begin to form around sides of pan. (Do not boil.) Pour into food processor, and pulse until smooth and glossy, about 4 times, stopping to scrape sides of bowl.
4. Pour ganache into prepared crust, and spread evenly to edges. Refrigerate until firm, at least 4 hours. Garnish with crystallized ginger, flaked coconut, and rosemary, if desired.

APPLE CUSTARD CAKE

MAKES 1 (9-INCH) CAKE

We love how pretty the thin slices of apple are on this sweet, custardy cake.

- 4 large eggs, room temperature and separated
- ¾ cup granulated sugar
- ½ cup unsalted butter, softened
- ¾ cup all-purpose flour
- 1 teaspoon apple pie spice
- 2 cups whole milk, lukewarm
- 1 teaspoon vanilla extract
- 3 medium apples, thinly sliced
- Honey or cane syrup, for drizzling
- Garnish: confectioners' sugar

1. Preheat oven to 325°.

2. Line a 9-inch square cake pan with parchment paper. Lightly spray with baking spray with flour.

3. In a medium bowl, beat egg yolks and granulated sugar with a mixer at medium speed until pale yellow and fluffy. With mixer on high speed, add butter, and beat for 2 minutes. With mixer on low speed, add flour and apple pie spice, beating until combined. Gradually add milk and vanilla, beating until combined.

4. In a clean bowl, using clean beaters, beat egg whites with a mixer at high speed until soft peaks form. Gently fold egg whites into batter in thirds. (Batter will be very thin.) Pour batter into prepared pan. Gently place apple slices in rows to top.

5. Bake until light golden brown around the edges, 50 minutes to 1 hour. Let cool completely. Serve with a drizzle of honey or cane syrup. Garnish with confectioners' sugar, if desired.

KITCHEN TIP This cake can be made up to 2 days in advance.

APPLE ROSE CAKE

MAKES 1 (8-INCH) CAKE

While we can't get over this stunning apple rose topping, we love the tender, gently spiced cake underneath even more.

- ½ cup unsalted butter, softened
- ½ cup granulated sugar
- 2 cups all-purpose flour
- 1½ teaspoons baking powder
- ¾ teaspoon apple pie spice
- ½ teaspoon kosher salt
- 3 large eggs
- ½ cup sour cream
- 1¼ teaspoons vanilla extract, divided
- 4 Pink Lady apples, cored, halved, and sliced ⅛ inch thick
- 1½ cups heavy whipping cream
- ½ cup confectioners' sugar

1. Preheat oven to 375°.

2. Spray an 8-inch round cake pan with baking spray with flour. Cut 2 (12x2-inch) strips of parchment paper and set in pan, perpendicular to each other and allowing the excess paper to hang over the edge of the pan.

3. In a large bowl, beat butter and granulated sugar with a mixer at medium speed until fluffy, 3 to 4 minutes, stopping to scrape sides of bowl.

4. In a medium bowl, whisk together flour, baking powder, apple pie spice, and salt. In a small bowl, whisk together eggs, sour cream, and 1 teaspoon vanilla. With mixer on low speed, gradually add flour mixture to butter mixture alternately with egg mixture, beginning and ending with flour mixture, beating just until combined after each addition. Spoon batter into prepared pan, smoothing top with an offset spatula. Starting on the outer rim and spiraling into center, arrange apple slices, skin side up, on top of batter.

5. Bake until a wooden pick inserted in center comes out clean, 30 to 35 minutes, loosely covering with foil after 15 minutes of baking to prevent excess browning. Let cool in pan for 15 minutes. Using the parchment as handles, carefully lift cake from pan.

6. In a small bowl, whisk together cream, confectioners' sugar, and remaining ¼ teaspoon vanilla until smooth. Drizzle glaze over cake. Serve warm or at room temperature.

CHOCOLATE MAYONNAISE CAKE

MAKES 1 (13X9-INCH) CAKE

Replacing eggs with mayonnaise in the batter–an old Southern trick–gives this cake an airy yet moist texture.

FOR CAKE

- **1 cup mayonnaise,* room temperature**
- **1 cup whole milk, room temperature**
- **2 teaspoons vanilla extract**
- **2 cups all-purpose flour**
- **1 cup granulated sugar**
- **¼ cup Dutch process cocoa powder**
- **2 teaspoons baking soda**

FOR CHOCOLATE FROSTING

- **1½ cups unsalted butter, softened**
- **½ teaspoon kosher salt**
- **4 cups confectioners' sugar, divided**
- **2 tablespoons whole milk, divided**
- **¾ cup chopped semisweet chocolate, melted and slightly cooled**

Garnish: chopped toasted pecans, chocolate curls (see Kitchen Tip)

1. Preheat oven to 350°.
2. Line a 13x9-inch baking pan with parchment paper, letting excess extend over sides of pan.

FOR CAKE

1. In a large bowl, whisk together mayonnaise, milk, and vanilla. In a medium bowl, whisk together flour, granulated sugar, cocoa, and baking soda. Gradually add flour mixture to mayonnaise mixture, stirring until well combined. Pour batter into prepared pan, smoothing top.
2. Bake until a wooden pick inserted in center comes out clean, 28 to 30 minutes. Let cool completely in pan on a wire rack. Using excess parchment as handles, remove from pan.

FOR CHOCOLATE FROSTING

1. In a large bowl, beat butter and salt with a mixer at medium speed until creamy, about 1 minute. Gradually add 2 cups confectioners' sugar and 1 tablespoon milk, beating until smooth, about 1 minute. Gradually add remaining 2 cups confectioners' sugar and remaining 1 tablespoon milk, beating until smooth and fluffy. Add melted chocolate, and beat until well combined and very fluffy, 3 to 5 minutes. Spread frosting onto cooled cake. Garnish with pecans and chocolate curls, if desired.

**We used Hellmann's Real Mayonnaise.*

KITCHEN TIP To create chocolate curls, microwave a chocolate block in 5-second intervals until slightly softened, about 10 seconds. Shave into curls using a Y-shaped peeler.

GINGERBREAD SHEET CAKE

MAKES 1 (13X9-INCH) CAKE

We used two types of molasses in this cake–unsulphured in the batter and sorghum as a finishing drizzle–for the perfect balance of rich sweetness.

FOR CAKE

- 1 cup unsalted butter, softened
- 1 cup firmly packed dark brown sugar
- 1 teaspoon vanilla extract
- 2 large eggs
- 3 cups all-purpose flour
- 2 teaspoons baking powder
- 2 teaspoons ground ginger
- 1 teaspoon ground cinnamon
- 1 teaspoon ground nutmeg
- ½ teaspoon baking soda
- ¼ teaspoon kosher salt
- 1 cup whole milk
- 1 cup unsulphured molasses
- ½ cup chopped crystallized ginger

FOR CREAM CHEESE FROSTING

- ¾ cup unsalted butter, softened
- 1½ (8-ounce) packages cream cheese, softened
- 6 cups confectioners' sugar
- ½ teaspoon vanilla extract
- ⅛ teaspoon kosher salt

Garnish: sorghum molasses, ground cinnamon

1. Preheat oven to 350°.
2. Spray a 13x9-inch baking pan with baking spray with flour. Line pan with parchment paper, letting excess extend over sides of pan.

FOR CAKE

1. In a large bowl, beat butter, brown sugar, and vanilla with a mixer at medium speed until creamy, 3 to 4 minutes, stopping to scrape sides of bowl. Add eggs, one at a time, beating well after each addition.
2. In a medium bowl, whisk together flour, baking powder, ground ginger, cinnamon, nutmeg, baking soda, and salt. In another medium bowl, whisk together milk and molasses. With mixer on low speed, gradually add flour mixture to butter mixture alternately with milk mixture, beginning and ending with flour mixture, beating just until combined after each addition. Stir in crystallized ginger. Spoon batter into prepared pan, spreading to edges.
3. Bake until a wooden pick inserted in center comes out clean, about 35 minutes. Let cool completely in pan. Using excess parchment as handles, remove cake from pan. Slide a metal spatula under cake to release from parchment. Place cake on a serving platter.

FOR CREAM CHEESE FROSTING

1. In a large bowl, beat butter and cream cheese with a mixer at medium speed until creamy. Gradually add confectioners' sugar, vanilla, and salt, beating until smooth. Cover and keep refrigerated until ready to use or up to 3 days; beat again for 30 seconds before using. Spread frosting onto cake. Just before serving, garnish with molasses and cinnamon, if desired.

BOURBON CARAMEL POUND CAKE

MAKES 1 (13-CUP) BUNDT CAKE

Topped with a Bourbon Caramel Sauce and infused with bourbon, this buttery cake gets spiked with a hint of cinnamon and orange, making it a total showstopper.

FOR POUND CAKE
- 1 cup unsalted butter, softened
- 1½ cups firmly packed light brown sugar
- ½ cup granulated sugar
- ½ teaspoon packed orange zest
- 4 large eggs, room temperature
- 1 teaspoon vanilla extract
- 2⅔ cups all-purpose flour
- 1 teaspoon kosher salt
- ½ teaspoon ground cinnamon
- ¼ teaspoon baking soda
- ⅔ cup whole buttermilk, room temperature
- ¼ cup bourbon
- Bourbon Caramel Sauce (recipe follows)
- Garnish: chopped candied pecans

FOR BOURBON CARAMEL SAUCE
- ½ cup firmly packed light brown sugar
- ⅓ cup dark corn syrup
- 2½ tablespoons whole buttermilk
- 2 tablespoons unsalted butter, cubed and softened
- ¼ teaspoon kosher salt
- 1½ teaspoons bourbon
- ¼ teaspoon vanilla extract

1. Preheat oven to 325°.

FOR POUND CAKE

1. In a large bowl, beat butter, sugars, and zest with a mixer at medium speed until fluffy, 3 to 4 minutes, stopping to scrape sides of bowl. Add eggs, one at a time, beating well after each addition. Beat in vanilla.

2. In a medium bowl, whisk together flour, salt, cinnamon, and baking soda. In a small bowl, whisk together buttermilk and bourbon. With mixer at low speed, gradually add flour mixture to butter mixture alternately with buttermilk mixture, beginning and ending with flour mixture, beating just until combined after each addition.

3. Generously spray a 13-cup cast-iron Bundt pan with baking spray with flour. Spread batter into prepared pan. Gently tap pan on a towel-lined countertop several times to release air bubbles.

4. Bake until a wooden pick inserted near center comes out clean, about 1 hour. Let cool in pan for 30 minutes. Invert cake onto a wire rack to remove, and let cool completely.

5. Transfer cake to a serving plate; drizzle with Bourbon Caramel Sauce. Garnish with candied pecans, if desired.

FOR BOURBON CARAMEL SAUCE

1. In a small enamel-coated cast-iron Dutch oven, bring brown sugar, corn syrup, buttermilk, butter, and salt to a boil over medium-high heat, stirring constantly. Cook, stirring constantly, for 2 minutes.

2. Remove from heat; stir in bourbon and vanilla. Pour sauce into a medium bowl, and let cool for 20 minutes before serving.

CHOCOLATE SOUR CREAM POUND CAKE

MAKES 1 (13-CUP) BUNDT CAKE

Don't have a cast-iron Bundt pan? You can bake this deliciously moist cake in a traditional 12- to 15-cup Bundt pan using the same oven temperature and baking time.

- **1¼ cups unsalted butter, softened**
- **3 cups granulated sugar**
- **2 teaspoons vanilla extract**
- **1 teaspoon almond extract**
- **6 large eggs**
- **3 cups all-purpose flour**
- **½ cup unsweetened cocoa powder**
- **½ teaspoon baking soda**
- **½ teaspoon kosher salt**
- **1 (8-ounce) container sour cream, room temperature**
- **⅓ cup chopped bittersweet chocolate, melted and slightly cooled**
- **2 tablespoons confectioners' sugar**

1. Preheat oven to 325°. Spray a 13-cup cast-iron Bundt pan with baking spray with flour.

2. In a large bowl, beat butter, granulated sugar, and extracts with a mixer at medium speed until fluffy, 3 to 4 minutes, stopping to scrape sides of bowl. Add eggs, one at a time, beating well after each addition.

3. In a medium bowl, whisk together flour, cocoa, baking soda, and salt. With mixer on low speed, gradually add flour mixture to butter mixture alternately with sour cream, beginning and ending with flour mixture, beating just until combined after each addition. Add melted chocolate, beating just until combined. Spoon batter into prepared pan, smoothing top with a spatula. Gently tap pan on counter twice to release air bubbles.

4. Bake until a wooden pick inserted near center comes out clean, about 1 hour and 15 minutes. Let cool in pan for 30 minutes. Remove from pan, and let cool completely on a wire rack. Sprinkle with confectioners' sugar.

ULTIMATE HUMMINGBIRD LAYER CAKE

MAKES 1 (9-INCH) CAKE

With its luscious, fruit-filled layers and generous dose of creamy frosting, this classic cake won't last long.

FOR CAKE

- 3 cups all-purpose flour
- 1 cup granulated sugar
- 1 cup firmly packed light brown sugar
- 1 teaspoon baking soda
- 1 teaspoon kosher salt
- 3 large eggs, room temperature and lightly beaten
- 1 cup canola oil
- 1 (8-ounce) can crushed pineapple in juice
- 2 cups mashed banana
- 1 cup chopped pecans, lightly toasted

FOR CREAM CHEESE FROSTING

- 2 (8-ounce) packages cream cheese, softened
- 1 cup unsalted butter, softened
- 7 cups confectioners' sugar, sifted
- 1 teaspoon vanilla extract

Garnish: chopped pecans

1. Preheat oven to 350°.
2. Line the bottoms of 2 (9-inch) round cake pans with parchment paper. Spray with baking spray with flour.

FOR CAKE

1. In a large bowl, whisk together flour, sugars, baking soda, and salt. Add eggs and oil, whisking until combined. Add pineapple with juice, banana, and pecans, stirring until combined. Divide batter between prepared pans.
2. Bake until a wooden pick inserted in center comes out clean, about 35 to 40 minutes. Let cool in pans for 10 minutes. Remove from pans, and let cool completely on wire racks.

FOR CREAM CHEESE FROSTING

1. In a large bowl, beat cream cheese and butter with a mixer at medium-high speed until smooth. Add confectioner's sugar, 1 cup at a time, beating at medium-low until combined, scraping sides of bowl with a rubber spatula before each addition. Add vanilla, beating until smooth. Using an offset spatula, spread 2 cups frosting on one cake layer; top with remaining cake layer. Spread 2 cups frosting on top of cake. Spread remaining 1 cup frosting onto sides of cake. (Frosting will be thin.) Using a bench scraper or clean offset spatula, apply gentle pressure around sides of cake, evening out frosting and removing any excess. (Cake sides should be visible through frosting.) Garnish with pecans, if desired.

COCONUT CAKE CHEESECAKE

MAKES 1 (8-INCH) CAKE

This cake's creamy filling complements the crunch of the crust and coconut topping for one dreamy dish.

FOR CRUST

- 2 cups graham cracker crumbs
- 1 cup sweetened flaked coconut
- ½ cup salted butter, melted

FOR FILLING

- 2 (8-ounce) packages cream cheese, softened
- 1 cup sugar
- 3 large eggs
- 2 cups sour cream
- 1 teaspoon fresh lime juice
- 1 teaspoon vanilla extract

FOR TOPPING

- ½ cup sweetened condensed milk
- ¼ cup coconut milk
- 1¼ cups sweetened flaked coconut
- ½ teaspoon vanilla extract

1. Preheat oven to 325°.

FOR CRUST

1. For crust: In a medium bowl, stir together graham cracker crumbs, coconut, and melted butter. Press evenly into the bottom and 1 inch up the sides of an 8-inch springform pan. Refrigerate for 10 minutes. Wrap foil tightly around bottom of springform pan.

FOR FILLING

1. In a large bowl, beat cream cheese and sugar with a mixer at medium speed until fluffy. Add eggs, one at a time, beating just until combined after each addition. Add sour cream, lime juice, and vanilla, beating until well combined. Pour into prepared crust.

2. Place springform pan in a large roasting pan. Add boiling water to roasting pan to a depth halfway up sides of springform pan.

3. Bake until center of cheesecake is set but jiggles slightly in the middle, about 1 hour and 15 minutes. Carefully remove cheesecake from roasting pan, and let cool completely on a wire rack. Refrigerate overnight.

FOR TOPPING

1. In a small bowl, stir together condensed milk, coconut milk, coconut, and vanilla. Top cheesecake with mixture. Chill until ready to serve.

BOURBON CRÈME BRÛLÉE

MAKES 6 SERVINGS

A hint of bourbon paired with a velvety crème brûlée is nothing short of perfection for this well-balanced dessert.

- **3 cups heavy whipping cream**
- **1 teaspoon vanilla extract**
- **5 large egg yolks, room temperature**
- **1 cup plus 4 tablespoons sugar, divided**
- **¼ cup bourbon**
- **¼ teaspoon kosher salt**

1. Preheat oven to 325°. Place 6 (8-ounce) ramekins in a 13x9-inch baking pan.
2. In a medium saucepan, heat cream and vanilla over low heat until bubbles form around sides of pan. (Do not boil.)
3. In a medium bowl, whisk together egg yolks, 1 cup sugar, bourbon, and salt until frothy, about 2 minutes.
4. Slowly whisk one-fourth of hot cream mixture into egg yolk mixture. Gradually add remaining hot cream mixture, gently whisking until combined. (Don't overmix or whisk too aggressively, as that will add too many air bubbles to the mixture.) Strain custard through a fine-mesh sieve into a large liquid-measuring cup. Divide mixture among ramekins. Pour hot water (161°) about three-fourths of the way up sides of pan, being careful not to get water into custard. Tightly cover pan with foil.
5. Bake until custard is set but jiggly, about 1 hour. Carefully remove ramekins from water, and let cool completely on a wire rack. Refrigerate until cold, about 4 hours, or up to overnight.
6. Sprinkle 2 tablespoons sugar (1 teaspoon each) onto custards; using a handheld kitchen torch, carefully brown sugar. Sprinkle remaining 2 tablespoons sugar (1 teaspoon each) onto custards; using a handheld kitchen torch, carefully brown sugar. (This will make sure you get a thick crust without burning or overheating the custard.) Serve immediately.

BLUEBERRY MERINGUES

MAKES 12

These pretty swirled treats are delightfully fruity and crisp.

FOR BLUEBERRY JAM
- **1 pound fresh blueberries**
- **1¼ cups sugar**
- **1 tablespoon fresh lemon juice**

FOR MERINGUES
- **4 large egg whites, room temperature**
- **¼ teaspoon cream of tartar**
- **⅛ teaspoon kosher salt**
- **1 cup sugar**
- **1 tablespoon cornstarch**
- **½ teaspoon vanilla extract**

Sweetened whipped cream, to serve

FOR BLUEBERRY JAM

1. In a medium saucepan, bring all ingredients to a boil over high heat. Reduce to medium-low, and simmer for 45 minutes. Transfer to a heatproof jar, and let stand until cool. Cover and refrigerate for up to 1 month.

FOR MERINGUES

1. Preheat oven to 225°. Line 2 large baking sheets with parchment paper.

2. In a microwave-safe dish, microwave ½ cup Blueberry Jam until just warm, about 30 seconds. Pour through a fine-mesh sieve into a bowl, discarding solids. Set aside.

3. In the bowl of a stand mixer fitted with the whisk attachment, beat egg whites at medium-high speed until foamy, about 1 minute. Add cream of tartar and salt, beating until combined.

4. In a medium bowl, whisk together sugar and cornstarch. With mixer on medium speed, gradually add sugar mixture to egg white mixture, 1 tablespoon at a time, beating until mixture is glossy and sugar is dissolved, 1 to 2 minutes. Increase mixer speed to high, and beat until stiff peaks form, 4 to 5 minutes. Beat in vanilla and ½ teaspoon warmed Blueberry Jam.

5. Spoon meringue by ⅓ cupfuls onto prepared pans. Spoon about ¼ teaspoon warmed Blueberry Jam over each meringue, and swirl with a small knife.

6. Bake for 2 hours. Turn oven off, and let meringues stand in oven with door closed for 12 hours. Serve with whipped cream and additional Blueberry Jam.

index